Michael Georg Grasser

Secure CPU

Michael Georg Grasser

Secure CPU

A Secure Processor Architecture for Embedded Systems

VDM Verlag Dr. Müller

Imprint

Bibliographic information by the German National Library: The German National Library lists this publication at the German National Bibliography; detailed bibliographic information is available on the Internet at http://dnb.d-nb.de.

Cover image: www.purestockx.com

Publisher:
VDM Verlag Dr. Müller Aktiengesellschaft & Co. KG , Dudweiler Landstr. 125 a, 66123 Saarbrücken, Germany,
Phone +49 681 9100-698, Fax +49 681 9100-988,
Email: info@vdm-verlag.de

Zugl.: Graz, Graz University of Technology, Dissertation, 2007

Produced in USA and UK by:
Lightning Source Inc., La Vergne, Tennessee, USA
Lightning Source UK Ltd., Milton Keynes, UK
BookSurge LLC, 5341 Dorchester Road, Suite 16, North Charleston, SC 29418, USA

ISBN: 978-3-639-02783-9

Contents

4

List of Figures

List of Abbreviations

ACC..................... Access Permissions

ALU .... Arithmetic Logical Unit

API .... Application Programming Interface

BCC..................... Bounds Check GNU C Compiler

BIT....................... Bitstream File (Binary Data File)

BSS .... Block Started by Symbol

CASH .... Checking Array bound violation using Segmentation HW

CIL....................... Common Intermediate Language

CP .... Co-Processor

CPLD................... Complex Programmable Logic Device

CPU..................... Central Processing Unit

CRED .... C Range Error Detector

CWP..................... Current Window Pointer

DAC..................... Digital To Analogue Converter

DCM .... Digital Clock Manager

DEP..................... Data Execution Protection

DSU..................... Debug Support Unit

DTD..................... Document Type Definition

EBP .... Enhanced Base Pointer

EDAC .... Error Detection And Correction

EEPROM............. Electrically Erasable Programmable Read-Only Memory

EIP .... Extended Instruction Pointer

ET........................ Enable Traps

EVP .... Enhanced Virus Protection

10

EX .... Execute

FP....................... Frame Pointer

FPGA .... Field Programmable Gate Array

FPU .... Floating Point Unit

GCC .... GNU C Compiler

GOT .... Global Offset Table

GPR .... General Purpose Registers

HTML .... HyperText Markup Language

HSAP .... Hardware/Software Address Protection

I/O .... Input/Output

ID......................... Instruction Decode

ISA .... Instruction Set Architecture

IU......................... Integer Unit

JTAG .... Joint Test Action Group

LAN .... Local Area Network

LDT .... Local Descriptor Table

LED .... Light Emitting Diode

LIFO .... Last In First Out

LSB .... Least Significant Bit

LUT .... Look-Up Table

MAC .... Media Access Control

MMU................... Memory Management Unit

NPC..................... Next Program Counter

NTSC .... National Television Systems Committee

NX .... No Execute

PAL .... Phase Alternation Line

PC .... Program Counter

PHY .... Physical Layer

PPN .... Physical Page Number

PSR .... Process State Register

PTD .... Page Table Descriptor

PTE .... Page Table Entry

PTP .... Page Table Pointer

RAD .... Return Address Defender

RAM .... Random Access Memory

RAR .... Return Address Repository

RISC .... Reduced Instruction Set Computing

SDRAM .... Synchronous Dynamic RAM

SJMP .... Secure Jump

SP .... Stack Pointer

SRAM .... Static RAM

SSP .... Stack-Smashing Protector

SVF .... Serial Vector Format

UCF .... User Constraints File

USB .... Universal Serial Bus

VHD .... VHDL Source Code File

VHDL .... Very High-Speed Hardware Description Language

XD .... Execute Disable

XML .... extensible Markup Language

Abstract

Embedded technologies are one of the fastest growing sectors in information technology today and they are still open fields with many business opportunities. Hardly any new product reaches the market without embedded systems components any more. However, main technical challenges include the design and integration, as well as providing the necessary degree of security especially when human safety can be influenced by the embedded system.

In the short term, the main idea of this book focuses the evaluation of methods for the improvement of code-security through measurements in hardware that can be transparent to software-developers. Therefore, the ideas of this work improve the security level in every system passively, with minor changes in hardware only. As numerically, most systems run on dedicated hardware and not on high-performance general purpose processors. There certainly exists a market even for new hardware to be used in real applications. Thus, the experience from the related project work can lead to valuable and marketable results for businesses and academics.

The book "Secure CPU" complies in its core issues the requirements of future commercial applications in very promising market segments. The project can be regarded as development tool for specialized architectures on the one hand and as user-transparent improvement in security for embedded systems based on standard intermediate code on the other hand. The performed changes are compliant to legacy software applications, as well as existing operating systems. Basically, a full compliance to the SPARC V8 reference architecture could be reached with the newly developed secure processor core.

1. Introduction

This book deals with the solution of an important problem in today's computer economy and industry. Buffer overflows are very common and only a few solutions are available yet, but they do not satisfy the actual needs. In the introductory chapter the current situation, as well as the project phases and the structure are described.

1.1. Current Situation

In November 1988, many organizations had to cut themselves off from the Internet, because of the *Morris worm*, which was a program to attack VAX and Sun machines. By some estimates, this program took down ten per cent of the entire Internet. In July 2001 another worm, named *Code Red*, eventually exploited over 300,000 computers worldwide, running Microsoft's Internet Information Service Web Server. In January 2003, the worm *Slammer* exploited vulnerability in Microsoft SQL Server software, disabling parts of the Internet in South Korea and Japan, disrupting Finnish phone service, as well as slowing many United States airline reservation systems, credit card networks and automatic teller machines. All of these attacks exploited a vulnerability called buffer overflow. An informal survey in 1999 on *Bugtraq*, which is a mailing list discussing security vulnerabilities, found out that two-third of the participants believed that the number one cause of vulnerabilities was buffer overflows. From January 1997 to March 2002, half of all security alerts from the CERT/CC were based on buffer overflow vulnerabilities. [1]

1.2. Project Phases

The research was organized in several project phases: The first was the evaluation and architecture design phase, in which the hardware and software architecture was created. This included the development and refinement of hardware and software models, as well as the evaluation of existing and appropriate optimisation methods.

The implementation phase dealt with the implementation of the design into a simulator. Several simulators for different purposes, as well as a complete tool-chain were evaluated and changed for the particular implementation. However, new simulator components had to be developed and various existing to be altered. Finally the hardware implementation in Very High-Speed Hardware Description Language (VHDL) had to be realised. Therefore, an existing processor core had to be altered to reflect the modified architecture and to be compatible to a common instruction set.

In the integration and test phase all components were integrated into the overall prototype. Several case studies were conducted in order to evaluate the approach. Project documentation and dissemination was conducted throughout the whole project. After each phase a project report was prepared and the scientific results were presented at international conferences. Some important work especially in the first phase had already been performed at the institute. Furthermore, clearly defined work packages were carried out in form of student projects.

1.3. Structure

The book "Secure CPU" is structured into six main chapters and includes an abstract, a list of contents, a list of figures and a list of abbreviations, as well as the acknowledgement at the beginning.

Chapter one represents the introduction, which includes the current situation at today's market, the necessary project phases to realise such a project and a short explanation of the structure.

Details about attack mechanisms are described in chapter two. After a rough explanation of the concepts of buffer overflows, the mechanisms of stack-smashing are presented. After the discussion of some historical attack prevention mechanisms, like StackGuard, Stack-Smashing Protector and Bound Checking, important state-of-the-art attack prevention techniques, like CASH and HSDefender, follow.

Chapter three deals with fundamental ideas of designing attack resistant embedded computing systems. This includes secure bound checking, with the explanation of different checking methodologies, as well as the idea of register and instruction set extension. Furthermore, secure bound storage with the developed SecureTag technique is proposed. Finally, the secure exception handling section illustrates an overview of exception handling strategies with traps.

Chapter four contains the proof of concept. A simulator engine was modified to verify, whether the new approaches in chapter three are valid. For that reason, the evaluation of processor simulators, the design and the modification of the simulator engine with associated performance results are included in this chapter.

The whole system configuration is discussed in chapter five. Firstly, the configuration of the SPARC V8 based processor core LEON 2 is described. Secondly, the necessary steps for a successful synthesis are presented. Finally, the development boards, XSV800 and GR-XC3S-1500, as well as the connection to the personal computer interfaces and synthesis of those are discussed in detail.

Chapter six includes some historical proposals and the developed implementation of secure bound checking. Moreover, the actual usage of secure bound storage in the selected software environment and processor architecture is discussed. Finally, the secure exception handling section describes the trap handling mechanisms in the target processor core.

A conclusion, containing a short summary of the project, as well as references to associated scientific publications and a list of all references are located at the end.

2. Related Work

In this chapter basic principles of buffer overflow and stack-smashing attacks are discussed. Several state-of-the-art approaches, which use a combination of hardware/software based buffer overflow prevention, are evaluated due to their features and usability. Also historical techniques that use compiler based prevention or a special memory marking technique for code execution protection, are discussed in this chapter. The results of this literature review are used as fundamental information to build up a secure processor architecture.

2.1. Attack Mechanisms

Many different mechanisms exist that try to attack several types of computer systems. These attacks can also be used to affect embedded systems. This section deals with the explanation of buffer overflow and stack-smashing attacks to understand the basic behaviours.

2.1.1. Buffer Overflows

In computer programming, a buffer overflow is an anomalous condition where a program somehow writes data beyond the allocated end of a buffer in memory. Since buffers are created to contain a finite amount of data, the extra information can overrun into adjacent buffers, corrupting or overwriting the valid data held in them. Although it may occur through programming errors, buffer overflows are increasingly common types of security attacks on data integrity. In buffer overflow attacks, the extra data may contain code designed to trigger specific actions or corrupt the control flow, in effect executing instructions from injected code or damaging existing data with confidential information. The number of buffer overflow attacks is increased, because several programming language supplied frameworks, which are not memory-safe and do not check unsafe programming styles. [2]

2.1.2.   Stack-Smashing

Stack-smashing is one of the most used attacks, which can be traced back to buffer overflows. This attack method is based on the corruption of the procedure return address in the memory stack. The memory stack is typically implemented as a contiguous block of memory that grows from higher addresses toward lower addresses. The end of the stack is marked by the Stack Pointer (SP), which is handled by the processor. The stack is divided into frames. Each of these frames belongs to a corresponding procedure. The Frame Pointer (FP) is used to mark the beginning of a frame. Since the procedure calls occur in a Last In First Out (LIFO) fashion, the currently used procedure is always on top of the stack.

If a procedure *f()* calls a procedure *g(s1, s2)*, the processor will transfer the control from *f()* to *g(s1, s2)*. Therefore, a new stack frame is added to the stack. Before the new SP is set, the FP is saved. This is necessary for restoring the old SP, when the frame is removed. Next the parameters *s1* and *s2*, the return address and the local variables have to be set. The parameters will be stored at the beginning of the frame, where the FP is located. Next the return address, which points to the next instruction of *f()*, and the saved FP are placed. At the end of the frame the local variables are located. When returning to *f()* the SP is set to the value of the FP and the old FP is restored. Next the frame is removed and the processor will jump to the given return address, where the execution of *f()* can be continued. [3, 4, 5]

The execution of this code sample starts with function *f()*. At this time there is only the stack frame of *f()* placed on the stack. Next, the function *g(s1, s2)* is called and a second frame is added. *s1* and *s2* are character pointers, which point to an array of characters. In the function *g(s1, s2)* two local variables are defined, one integer *a* and an array of one hundred characters *buf*. Next, the function *strcpy()* is called. This function copies a character string from *s1* to *buf*, without checking the sizes of the arguments. If the size of *s1* is greater than *buf* a buffer overflow happens and other entries of the stack frame, like the FP and the return address, are being overwritten.

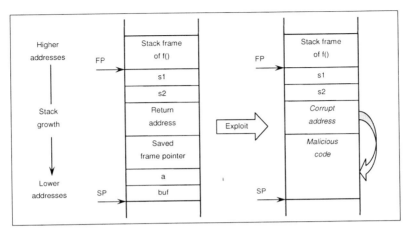

Figure 2-1: Buffer overflow attack via an exploit

The stack layout in the right of Figure 2-1 visualises a possible affect of an exploit. An attacker will use this malfunction to inject malicious code and to execute it afterwards. To perform stack-smashing, a buffer overflow condition has to be initiated and the return address has to be changed in a way that it points to injected, malicious code. The code sample, shown in Figure 2-2, is considered to demonstrate the behaviour of a buffer overflow. [4]

```
01      int f() {
02              ...
03              g(s1, s2);
04              ...
05      }
06
07      int g(char *s1, char *s2) {
08              int a;
09              char buf[100];
10              ...
11              strcpy(buf, s1);
12      }
```

Figure 2-2: Code sample for a buffer overflow attack

2.2. Historical Attack Prevention Mechanisms

There are several possible levels, where a defence mechanism can be inserted. Firstly, changes in the programming language can be made at language level to reduce the risk of buffer overflows. Secondly at source code level, static or dynamic source code analysers can be deployed to check the code for buffer overflow problems. Thirdly, a change in the compiler can implement bound checking and can protect certain addresses from being overwritten. Furthermore, rules for memory pages were invented that allow a separation of non-executable and executable content, but these rules can only be changed at operating system level. Finally, techniques for protecting systems against attacks can partly be implemented in hardware.

2.2.1.   StackGuard

The idea is to place a control value, the so called canary, in front of the saved return address. If a buffer overflow occurs, this value will be overwritten. So the buffer overflow can be detected and the program will be terminated. A problem is that there is a possibility for attackers to guess the canary value. If the canary value is chosen right during the attack, a buffer overflow can not be recognized. If the memory image of a running process can be examined, it will be successful in finding even a canary initialised with a random value.

StackGuard is only of historical interest. It was developed by Immunix in 1997 and was the first tool, which tried to prevent attacks. Unfortunately there are no updates any more, but this project is important, because it was the origin for many other projects to prevent buffer overflows. StackGuard is a simple C compiler patch that changes GNU C Compiler (GCC) functions, which are responsible for the prologue and epilogue respectively. In earlier versions another feature, called MemGuard, was added to StackGuard. Its main idea was to set the saved return address read-only, but due to performance reasons this feature was removed in later versions. One weakness of StackGuard is that the canary is placed before the return address. For this reason the other components in the stack frame, like local variables or the FP are not protected from getting overwritten. [6]

In later versions of StackGuard the canary was placed before the FP, but local variables were still unprotected. Firstly, the canary was a NUL-Canary (0x00000000) because an attacker could not forge this value, using string operations. The second approach was a terminator-canary, which consisted of

NUL (0x00), LF (0X0a), EOF (0xFF) and CR (0x0d). This canary was hard to forge, because almost every string operation terminates. [7]

2.2.2. Stack-Smashing Protector

The Stack-Smashing Protector (SSP), former known as ProPolice, is also based on the concept of StackGuard, but has also many new features. SSP is an IBM product, which is integrated in GCC since version 4.1. It was implemented using the intermediate code translator of GCC, because there was only one exit point per function and the location of each variable have been decided. A random canary was chosen, which was implemented through the Linux random number generator located at */dev/urandom* or */dev/random*. In SSP a new safety function model was introduced that changes the stack layout. Three methods were implemented for stack saving:

- A canary value is placed before the FP

- Change the order of the local variables. Character variables that are vulnerable are placed between the canary and the other variables.

- Copies of the arguments are made and are put, under consideration of the second method, to the locals. These copies are used instead of the original parameters.

Through these three methods it was really hard for attackers to succeed in taking control of a program. There are also limitations of this method. The pointer variable can not be protected in a structure that includes a pointer variable and a character array, because changing the variable order is prohibited. It protects only the stack, but the heap is unprotected and that is why dynamically allocated character arrays could still be used for buffer overflows. Functions, which call trampoline code, are also not protected. There is another limitation on keeping pointer variables safe. It is when an argument is declared as variable, which is used by a function with a varying number of arguments of varying types. The usage of pointer variables can be determined at execution only. But nevertheless, SSP is currently one of the best compiler-based solutions. [8]

2.2.3.   Microsoft /GS Compiler Option

Microsoft has developed a compiler flag that acts similarly to StackGuard. This feature is provided per default by Visual Studio .NET and would cause a false sense of security for the developers, because it can easily get defeated. A random-canary is used in this concept and saved in the *.data* segment. This fact is a potential weakness, because the attack would be successful, when a variable and the canary in the *.data* segment are over flown. Another weakness is that a function pointer that points to the security handler is also stored in the *.data* segment. Even if no security handler has been defined there is still a part of code that is executed by the process. The default steps taken if the cookies do not match are to set the *UnhandledExceptionFilter* to 0x00000000 and call the *UnhandledExceptionFilter* function afterwards. This will shutdown the particular process immediately. [9]

There are several well known approaches, which are not based on StackGuard that compiler-producers might use to defeat buffer overflow attacks. Microsoft chose to adopt a weak solution rather than a more robust solution. This is a design-level flaw leading to a very serious set of potential attacks against code compiled with the Microsoft compiler. [10]

2.2.4.   Bounds Checking

The main reason for the buffer overflow problem is that in C based programming languages bound checking is not implemented. For this reason it is necessary that programmers do these checks manually. Therefore, Paul Kelly and Richard Jones have developed a concept that checks automatically array and pointer de-references by a GCC extension. This work was published in [11]. The extension provides a complete bound checking mechanism for C programs, which is able to prevent successfully *out-of-bounds* write access. Programs compiled with this patch are compatible with ordinary GCC modules, because they have not changed the representation of pointers. Rather, they derive a base pointer from each pointer expression and check the attributes of that pointer to determine whether the expression is within-bounds. Since the slowdown is proportionate to pointer usage, which is quite common in privileged programs, the performance penalty is particularly unfortunate. [12]

An object table is used that represents a run-time data structure storing all base addresses and sizes of objects. With this information it is easier to determine, if an address is out-of-bounds. For performance reasons this object table is implemented as a splay tree. Every de-reference operation for a call to a function is substituted in a special checking library. Another feature is that this tool provides a bound checked version of all functions of the C standard library. A noticeable weakness is that this concept can not operate, when an out-of-bounds pointer is used to compute an in-bound pointer. Unfortunately this case happens quite often.

Therefore, the C Range Error Detector (CRED) was developed, which was published in [13]. Every out-of-bounds pointer value is replaced by an out-of-bounds object that is created for that particular value. The actual pointer value and the information on the referent are stored in this object. These objects are not entered in the object table, but they are stored in a hash table. For security purposes, it is needed to check the bounds of string data and thus significantly reduces the overhead of securing software systems without compromising the quality of protection offered. The disadvantage of this technique is that an out-of-bounds write will be detected, but causes a termination of the program. Under consideration of the performance loss, this solution is not suitable for a usage in embedded computer systems.

In [14] each allocated memory block is associated with an unbounded size and so out-of-bounds accesses can be considered as programming errors. This approach is based on CRED and the idea is to modify the generated code in a way that it stores also the data in the hash table when out-of-bounds writes occur, instead of terminating the execution. When an out-of-bounds read occurs, the hash table is searched and if no suitable entry is found, a default value is returned. The hash table has a fixed size, because otherwise an attacker could succeed in doing a denial of service attack by causing so many out-of-bounds writes until no memory is left. So the hash table could be regarded as an out-of-bounds cache. The implemented replacement strategy is recently used. Boundless computing successfully eliminates the negative consequences of *out-of-bounds* errors and enables to execute the corresponding memory errors and as a result continuing to successfully process the given workload.

2.2.5. Return Address Defender

Return Address Defender (RAD), published in [15], is a compiler patch that automatically inserts protection code into target programs so that attackers can not get control of the program by overwriting any return address. RAD adds protection code in the functions prologues and epilogues. This technique makes a copy of all return addresses in a particular data segment, called Return Address Repository (RAR). The memory regions around the RAR are set read-only in a way that the repository is protected against overflows. Each time a function returns, the return address is checked with the copy in the RAR.

There exist two different versions of RAD: MineZone RAD and Read-Only RAD. MineZone RAD has a better performance, but Read-Only RAD is more secure. Considering MineZone RAD, the first instruction that is executed after a function call adds the return address to a global integer array, which is surrounded by read-only memory. This is implemented by the system call *mprotect()*, which sets memory locations directly before and after the RAD to read-only. In the function epilogue the return address on the stack is compared to the return address in the RAR. When they are equal the return address in the RAR is popped and the control is transferred to the calling function. When they are not equal the attacked program terminates. MineZone RAD does not protect against a *Direct Return Address Modification Attack*. Read-Only RAD sets the RAR simply read-only. The disadvantage is that if a function call occurs, the RAR must be set writeable again. This happens in the prologue of the function and after storing the RAR has to be set read-only again.

To conclude, changing of read-only flags in Read-Only RAD consumes more overhead, when compared to MineZone RAD, but offers more security. [16]

2.2.6. StackShield

StackShield uses the *Global-Ret-Stack* technique, which implements additional statements in the prologue and epilogue of the considered software functions. The idea is to place a copy of the return address in a location of the memory, which is not overflowable. In the epilogue both addresses are compared and if not equal, the address on the stack simply gets overwritten by the address on the *Global-Ret-Stack*. The assembler code generates a global array with the default size of 256 elements and two global pointers *retptr* and *rettop*. *Retptr* points to the first free element and *rettop* points to the last element of the array. In the prologue the two pointers are compared to determine the right place for saving the return address. In the epilogue a manipulation of the return address is not possible, because the original address is directly taken from the *Global-Ret-Stack* instead of the return address on the stack.

The second feature is the *Ret-Range-Check* method. When a program is executed a variable called *shielddatabase* is initialised in the Block Started by Symbol (BSS) segment. In every epilogue the return address is compared to the location of this variable. Fundamentally, it is expected that the return address points to the code segment, which means that the address is lower than the address of the variable. Every attempt to jump to an address higher than the address of the *shielddatabase* variable causes a termination of the program. The third feature includes the protection of function pointers. [17]

2.2.7. StackOFFence

The technique, which is proposed in [18], involves transforming or encrypting the instruction pointer value, residing in the Extended Instruction Pointer (EIP) register. The return address is encrypted before it is placed on the stack. The encryption is done efficiently by exclusive ORing the EIP with a unique key that can be generated in a fairly simple manner.

When affecting return from a function call, the encrypted EIP value is again exclusive ORed with this key to yield a true and correct value. In case of overwriting the encrypted return address, the decrypted address will point on a random destination. So, an attacker can basically not take control of the program. The key used for this technique should have some properties:

- It should not change during a function call.
- It should also be dynamic, so that an attacker is unable to guess it.
- It should be easy to create, due to performance reasons.

In [18], it was suggested to use the contents of the Enhanced Base Pointer (EBP) register as the key, because it fulfilled the criteria above. To avoid jumping to random return addressed after a buffer overflow, a second method was introduced. The unencrypted return address is also saved on the stack and if a function returns, it is compared to the decrypted return address. When they are not equal a buffer overflow attack has occurred and the control is given to a buffer overflow handling function. For the implementation of StackOFFence only small modifications should be necessary, which affect two functions of GCC that are responsible for the prologue and epilogue. Unfortunately, the proposed technique is only theoretical, because no implementation is currently available. However, it provides a good approach how to securely store return addresses with special encryption techniques.

2.2.8.   Conclusion

The historical attack prevention mechanisms are mostly implemented at the compiler level. Furthermore, several techniques secure function return addresses by encrypting and decrypting in a defined way or storing the return addresses in a special location. The described attack prevention mechanisms are currently obsolete. As a result, the usage is limited to historical legacy applications.

2.3. State-of-the-art Attack Prevention Mechanisms

This section contains noticeable state-of-the-art hardware/software prevention approaches. They should give a rough overview about existing designs on the market and should represent factors, which can be improved to invent a secure processor architecture. These approaches are partly comparable with the design, which will be discussed later in this work.

2.3.1. Protection from Code Execution at Data Regions

In conventional computer systems code and data is stored at the same memory location, which is called von-Neumann architecture. The named technique has enforced, because it has a simple structure and only one main memory is needed, where code and data is stored. Concerning buffer overflows, storing code and data at the same memory location is basically a bad decision, because it could be possible that data will be overwritten with malicious data. If the attacker manages to change the return address of the stack frame, it is possible to execute the inserted code. This method is called stack-smashing and was described in section 2.1.2.

If code and data are stored at physically separated memory locations, like in the Harvard architecture, it should not be possible to execute code at data regions. The reason therefore is that new code can not be inserted into code region after compilation. It has to be remarked that the possibility for a buffer overflow has not changed, but now only the data region of the separated memory is affected.

Several chip manufactures – such as AMD and Intel – have implemented a quasi separation of code and data. That technique does not use the Harvard architecture, because code and data are still stored at the same memory location. Instead of the physical separation a bit is added, which marks memory pages to be executable or not. If code is executed at data regions, it is recognized and the process will be terminated by an exception. Concluding, it should be possible to secure a computer system partly from the consequences of buffer overflows.

The idea of this technique was initially proposed from AMD, as well as Microsoft and was published in [19]. Researchers found out that the only way to definitively address this problem was to make physical changes in both the processor and the operating system. AMD had designed a special technique for their 64 bit processors, which is called Enhanced Virus Protection (EVP) and adds a bit called No Execute (NX). On the other hand Microsoft designed a software based technique called Data Execution Protection (DEP), which should work together with the NX bit from AMD. [20]

The NX bit specifically refers to the last bit in the paging table entry of an x86 processor. If this bit is set to 0, then code can be executed from that page; if set to 1, code cannot be executed from that page, and anything residing there is assumed to be only data. These pages have to conform to a special page table format, rather than the original page table format for x86.

Meanwhile Intel had designed a similar feature. They added to some of their processors (like Celeron D, Pentium 4 and Pentium D) a bit called Execute Disable (XD), which has the same functionality as the NX bit of AMD. [21] Both features – NX bit of AMD and XD bit of Intel – need the support of an operating system. The reason therefore is that the operating system has to assign the pages that are executable at memory allocation. Microsoft designed DEP, which is yet implemented at Microsoft Windows XP Service Pack 2, the 64 bit version of Windows XP and Windows Server 2003. If the processor determines a process, which wants to execute code at a data region, an exception is thrown. [22]

AMD is gaining support for a feature in its processors that helps to stop buffer overflow exploits. Firstly, a computer copies input data, which includes malicious code, into a buffer of the program stack. The data overflows the buffer and overwrites another stack. Data overwrites the original procedure return address to point to data in the buffer, which actually contains special processor instructions. When the process finishes, the return instruction transfers the control to the return address and thus to the buffer. The processor tries to execute the given instructions, which include the malicious code. AMDs new technology blocks execution of those instructions and the processor generates and exception to the operating system. The functionality is visualised in Figure 2-3. [19]

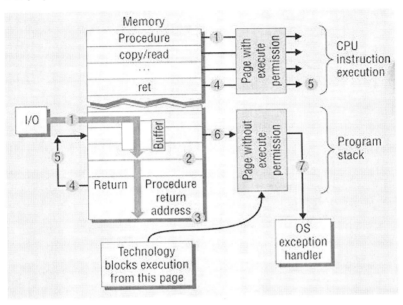

Figure 2-3: Execution protection of code at data regions [19]

Which processes are handled and how they are handled depend on the configuration of DEP and the mode – user or kernel mode – of the affected process? In case of user mode, the process causes a STATUS_ACCESS_ VIOLATION. In most processes this will be an unhandled exception and result in termination. Due to the weakness of some programs, DEP offers the possibility to exclude user mode programs of being handled. The handling of kernel mode processes is quite different. Firstly, there is no possibility to selectively exclude processes from being handled by DEP. Secondly, the parts of the stack that are handled depends on the version of Microsoft Windows. Considering 32 bit versions only the stack is handled, in 64 bit versions also an additional paged pool and a session pool are handled. A violation against DEP from a kernel mode process will result in a bug check.

Possible settings are shown in Figure 2-4. [22]

Setting	Description
OptIn	Windows system binaries and processes are handled by DEP.
OptOut	All processes are handled by DEP. There is a possibility to exclude user mode programs from handling.
AlwaysOn	All processes are handled by DEP. There is no possibility to exclude user mode programs from handling.
AlwaysOff	With this setting DEP is deactivated.

Figure 2-4: Various settings of DEP

There are also other operating systems, which support this technique. Particularly some Linux versions have already implemented a protection against overflow attacks. As an example, Debian developed a version of their release from i386 to the new generation of 64 bit processors, which can handle the NX bit. [23]

One of the problems of this new technique is the interaction of processor and operating system. If an attacker manages to get control of the operating system, it should also be possible to handle the setting of NX or XD bits. The reason for that is that this prevention technique operates at kernel mode, which means that an attacker could basically control everything. [24] The consequence of an attack is that the operating system may not correctly set the protection bits and so the processor may not detect an execution of code at data regions. In this context the possibility to exclude some processes from DEP has also to be mentioned.

To disable the NX/XD support for a process is determined at execution time. This is done by the routine *LdrpCheckNXCompatibility*, which are located at *ntdll.dll*. This routine checks if the NX or XD bits should be set. Furthermore, the operating system looks at the application database to check, whether DEP should be enabled or disabled. If an attacker manages to change the execution bits of the process that should be exploited, it also should also be possible to execute code at data regions. [25] Another thing that should be mentioned is that the NX and XD technique does not help against changing the return address of a function call. This address is also stored at the stack and as a consequence a buffer overflow can overwrite it. [20]

The NX and XD technique does not aim to protect the changes of the return addresses and so this has to be considered as a noticeable disadvantage. Another disadvantage is the fact that there exist processors on the market, where this technique is implemented, but not activated per default. Concluding, the NX and XD bit in combination with DEP can not provide a full buffer overflow protection. Several mechanisms have already been developed to attack this protection technique, because setting the NX or XD bit is also done via software and is therefore vulnerable to attacks.

2.3.2.   Checking Array Bound Violation

Checking Array bound violation using Segmentation Hardware (CASH) is a compiler approach like Bounds Check GNU C Compiler (BCC). But since BCC is not used because of its bad performance, CASH is trying to optimise bounds checking, so that hardly no overhead results. A high ambition knowing that the biggest problem of bounds checking technologies has always been the performance. A hardware that already exists in 90% of end-user computers is used to improve performance. The piece of hardware used is the virtual memory segmentation unit of Intel x86 processors. CASH allocates a new segment for each statically defined array or dynamically allocated pointer object. [26]

An important issue, when checking bounds of pointers, is to map the reference to the object itself. This is done by using a shadow pointer pointing to an objects information structure. The pointer and its shadow form a new structure, which is used throughout the source code. The information structure consists of three words and is situated directly behind the base address. The three words define low and high bound and the objects Local Descriptor Table (LDT) index. Whenever an array is allocated, CASH has to allocate an associated segment. Similarly, when an array is freed, the associated array is de-allocated.

Therefore, the *malloc()* and *free()* routines are modified to include the segment initialisation and clean-up steps. A disadvantage of the segment-based approach is that only less than 8192 objects can co-exist simultaneously in a segment. When more objects are needed CASH assigns a global segment and is essentially disabling the array bound checking for these objects. The Linux kernel 2.4 uses the system call *modify_ldt()* to add or remove an entry from the LDT. Switching from user to kernel space performs a change of LDT entries. This would lead to a high performance overhead. In case of normal usage of segments, switches happen more often, because every array is using its own segment. Therefore, a low overhead system call had to be developed. This better performance system call was made by use of a call gate, which is set up once and can then be used to call a *cash_modify_ldt* and resides in kernel space. [26]

For further optimisation all parameters are passed to this function through registers to eliminate the overhead of copying the parameters from user stack to the kernel stack. The second optimisation is to perform LDT entry allocation and de-allocation in user space. There is a *free_ldt_entry* list stored in user space, which maintains all free LDT entries. When a new segment was freed, its entry is just set *free*. It is not needed to change to kernel space for each freed entry. The set-free entry can be reused each time for a new segment. Another optimisation is that CASH keeps a 3 entry cache to store the three most recently freed segments. Whenever hardware bound checking is not possible, CASH can fall back to software array bound checking. This happens, when more than three arrays are involved within one loop. [26]

CASH is reported to be not as secure as BCC, because CASH only check bounds within loops. Since most of today's overflow attacks happen in loops this does not seem to be problematic. Furthermore, the CASH approach could be more usable than BCC, because of its better performance.

2.3.3.   Array and Pointer Bound Checking

Most array and pointer bound checking approaches were badly performing, so in this section faster techniques were proposed. In particular, there are two methods proposed in [27] which should, when combined, result in incredible performance. The change in software concerns only the data types pointer and array, as well as a new structure *template* is defined. This structure includes the pointer _value and two additional pointers _low_bound and _high_bound, where the associated bounds are stored. This new structure can deal either with insecure, which are not using bound checks or secure functions.

```
01      foo() {
02              int a[100];
03              int I;
04              int *p;
05              p = a;
06              for (i=0; i<=100; i++)
07                      *(p+i) = i;
08      }
```

Figure 2-5: Code sample without bound checking

The basic code sample [27] is shown in Figure 2-5, as well as the modified code sample [27] is illustrated in Figure 2-6. As theoretically discussed before, the modified code sample has an additional *typedef* structure, which represents a new pointer structure. This is also used in the procedure foo() to increase the security via bound checking.

```
01      typedef struct EPT_INT {
02              int *value;
03              int *low_bound;
04              int *high_bound;
05      } enhance_ptr_int;
06
07      foo() {
08              int i, a[100];
09              enhance_ptr_int _BP_a = {&a[0],&a[0],&a[99]};
10              enhance_ptr_int _BP_p;
11              _BP_p.value = a;
12              _BP_p.low_bound = &a[0];
13              _BP_p.high_bound = &a[99];
14
15              for (i=0; i<=100; i++)
16                      if(((_BP_p.value+i) < _BP_p.low_bound) ||
17                         ((_BP_p.value+i) > _BP_p.high_bound))
28                              exit(-1);
19                      *(_BP_p.value+i) = i;
20              }
21      }
```

Figure 2-6: Code sample with bound checking

An optimisation approach was used to minimize the necessary bound checks. Since *out-of-bounds* exceptions can only happen, when data is changed and written back to memory, only writing instructions have to be considered. This software bound check has to be compiled and transferred to microinstruction level, so a new bound check instruction has to be implemented. Using the DLX Architecture it was shown that four instructions were needed, which would result in six additional clock cycles per bound check. To implement all security features, additional hardware was needed, as shown in Figure 2-7. On the one hand this resulted in a larger Instruction Decode (ID) or Execute (EX) register and on the other hand a second Arithmetic Logic Unit (ALU) was needed to perform the comparison in parallel. Moreover, an additional gate, XORing them and determining an *out-of-bounds* exception was necessary. [27]

Fundamentally, it is a new idea, but also has drawbacks. One of those is the additional effort in software, which is needed to implement this technique. Furthermore, the source code of the user application has to be available and finally, limitations considering the DLX architecture are present.

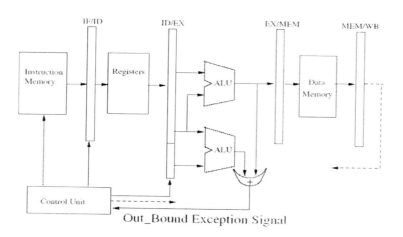

Figure 2-7: A second ALU and a bigger ID/EX register [27]

2.3.4. Hardware/Software Address Protection

There are many tools that defend against stack-based buffer overflows. Some tools even help in protecting the heap and the BSS. All need source code or special compilers to get the third-party components secured. Embedded systems have to fulfil certain requirements in latency, throughput, power consumption and more. In most cases no source code is available, therefore it is complicated to be sure about the related buffer overflow vulnerability.

This proposal tries to defend against both, stack-smashing and function pointer attacks. Each problem is solved by a different approach. Since stack-smashing attacks are easy and often carried out, a proper solution with less performance is needed. The Hardware/Software Address Protection (HSAP) is defending the stack by checking the addresses bounds. Since it is known that in the Intel x86 architecture, each of the endangered addresses is lower or equal to the FP, the system check them. When an address is in the danger area, the associated operation is not permitted. Therefore, variables that should be changed at runtime must be stored in the heap. For the reason of performance, the bound checking is done as an added phase – before the write phase – in the processor pipeline. If the bound check fails, the write operation is also not permitted. By this measure very little performance loss at a very high security level is guaranteed. Other danger areas are heap, BSS and Global Offset Table (GOT). These can be over flown by so called function pointer attacks. Most of current programs use dynamic binding when standard libraries are needed. The attack is carried out via overwriting the absolute position of a library in memory. Although this kind of attack requires further knowledge and so is done more seldom than the stack-smashing attack, it poses a problem that should not be ignored. [28]

The following approach, which was published in [27], tries to guarantee security by obscurity. The technique just tries to make pointer manipulation more difficult for attackers. Encryption of all pointer addresses improves security and in this case for each new process a random value is generated and stored in an additional register. A secure jump (SJMP) instruction with the following functionality was defined:

- When the address of a function to a function pointer is assigned, the address of the function is exclusive ORed with a key R and then the result is put into a function pointer.

- When the function is called using function pointers, SJMP is used.

Since the key is stored in a special register, its value cannot be overwritten by attacks. There are also problems arising, because the key value could be guessed or the registers value is sniffed when written to the special register.

2.3.5. Hardware/Software Defender

In [29], new techniques against stack-smashing attacks and for securing function pointers are proposed. The protection against buffer overflows by means of hardware/software solutions and the ability to check, if third-party developers have correctly implemented the protection mechanisms already existed. This issue seems to be very important, because of the trend in embedded system design, to use off-the-shelf components.

An extension, based on the two new instructions *SCALL* and *SRET*, which are counterparts to *CALL* and *RET*, had to be implemented. The idea is to secure the already existing instructions of executing, when the return address has been changed. This is done by generating a signature, XORing the return address with a random value. This random value is generated for each new process, when loaded into memory. For security reasons this key is stored into a register R. This is important to consider that the key has to be stored in memory, when a context switch to another process occurs. The necessary hardware is shown in Figure 2-8. [30]

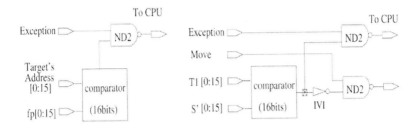

Figure 2-8: Hardware against stack-smashing [30]

SCALL and SRET were implemented, regarding to [29] as follows:

- Push the return address onto the stack.

- Generate a signature S by $S = XOR(R, Ret)$, where R stores the key and Ret represents the return address.

- Push signature S onto the stack.

- Jump to the target address, which is stored in Program Counter (PC)

- Load SP and $SP+4$ to two temporary registers, $T1$ and $T2$. These registers store S and Ret pushed in SCALL, respectively.

- Calculate $S' = XPR(R, T2)$.

- Compare $T1$ and S': If equal, move $T2$ to PC or otherwise, generate a stack overflow exception.

A problem comes up when thinking about the context switches. If the key is stored in memory, it can be read by an attacker. Although there should not be any security concern about that, I disagree. Suppose, that an attacker could inquire the key, it would be easier to break into the system again. Since the process can be restarted, the probability of a server restart and by the restart of the concerned application is high. This could lead to re-attacks. It is important to know that protection against internal users is not discussed here. External attackers can try to find the key by either trying all possible values or rebuilding an equal system.

Another protection mechanism against function pointer overflow is proposed in [30]. It also uses the key R and a good sharing of resources leads to better performance. Both types of jumps, direct and indirect are addressed. The protection of jump addresses is implemented by adding another secure instruction SJMP. Although its performance is worse than a pure hardware bound check, there are fewer requirements that have to be considered during implementation.

The Hardware/Software Defender, also called HSDefender, technique, proposed in [29], can defend against more types of buffer overflow attacks by combining its two components compared with previous work. Moreover, using its stack-smashing protection component, it can defend against stack-smashing attacks no matter what return addresses or FPs are used. HSDefender can defend against local function pointer attacks and shared function pointer table attacks in various places, which cannot be achieved by most of the previous work. Concluding, this work is noticeable, but does not fulfil all requirements to implement a secure architecture. Therefore, new approaches have to be developed.

2.3.6.   Conclusion

All state-of-the-art attack prevention mechanisms are worth to be discussed, but they face an important topic. The commercially available technique from AMD and Intel, which protects code execution at data regions, is matured and used in many computer systems. The CASH approach, which uses existing hardware components of existing processors, is easy to implement, but due to the fact that the segmentation hardware is not used very often, also the proposed implementation will not be used. Academic approaches, like to HSAP and HSDefender, are good proposals, but it will be hard to penetrate the market with a general change in a processor architecture without the support of processor manufacturers and a known common software environment. Concluding, there is a need in developing a secure processor architecture in addition to a secure software environment.

3. Design

This chapter describes the basic idea and the draft design of the system, as well as possibilities that exist to reach a proper solution. It is divided into secure bound checking, secure bound storage and secure exception handling sections.

3.1. Secure Bound Checking

The idea of preventing buffer overflows has bothered many computer architects. Most solutions of this security problem are based on a change in software. Before the compilation of source code a special pre-processor integrates compare statements into existing programs. The comparisons are carried out before array access and prevent the executed program from reading invalid data. This approach leads to better security, because each memory access is checked before the invalid data is transmitted to the processor. The big amount of additional instructions decreases system performance though. This disadvantage should be circumvented by an integration of the operation of comparison in hardware. There should be no need for an extra instruction, which triggers the comparison. The check should be done seamlessly in the background, without any necessity of interaction. Although the loading of bounds into registers cannot be omitted, this concept will lead to better performance and security.

3.1.1. Arithmetic Comparison

Arithmetic operations in processors are calculated by the Arithmetic Logical Unit (ALU). The arithmetic operation of comparing two values is like a normal subtraction. Therefore, each processor can carry out such comparisons out of the box. To trigger this operation, a pseudo-instruction has to be executed. This instruction calculates the difference between the two given input values. The difference to a common subtraction is that the result does not have to be stored permanently in a register. In fact, the outcome is needed for determination of equality or inequality. As soon as a result equals or is less than zero, it can be discarded. If the result is greater than zero, the inputs are in the provided range.

This logical value is reported to one of the Processor State Registers (PSR). At the beginning of the pipeline the processor has the possibility to take a branch or not and for that reason, the PSR has to be checked. If the *equal to zero* flag was not set, the comparison was not successful and the processor has to take an action.

3.1.2.   Hardware Comparison

Another concept for comparison at register transfer level would be the direct comparison of two register values. Direct means that there is no additional register, which is necessary to stores intermediate results. The operation should be done at once without the necessity of writing to a register. To realise this concept a special comparator unit have to be included into the processor core. It is directly linked to the General Purpose Registers (GPR), as input sources.

Firstly, the data is written to registers like in a normal ALU. Then a comparison is carried out by a number of gates. The number of gates matches the input bit width. Every bit of the two registers is checked for equality. The outcomes are combined and evaluated, whether they are true or false. Although there are two operations there is no delay, because the gates provide their result at once. The result is handed over to the exception handling through a single wire, being the comparators only output. The exception handling takes action and interrupts the execution.

3.1.3.   Evaluation of Concepts

The concept of bound checking requires two comparisons, because the current value must be checked on both sides to be in range. This results in one comparison against the lower and one additional comparison against the higher bound. To make bound checking more accepted, its performance must be increased. One approach is the parallelising of the two comparisons. For parallel execution parallel hardware structures must exist.

When using the arithmetic conception, there is no way around the integration of a second ALU. A big effort in hardware is necessary to realise this approach and this results in more expenses. A better way is to integrate a simpler concept, which requires less hardware to be added. The hardware comparator is designed of a small number of gates, which results in less hardware costs. Furthermore, its functionality is restricted to the operation of comparing. On the one hand, it is less powerful than an ALU, but on the other hand it can be integrated into the core at any place.

A further advantage is its flexibility. When merging two or more of these units, reams of comparisons can be done simultaneously. Since the hardware comparator is not integrated into the normal pipeline, it does not need a complete pipeline cycle to deliver the result. Though, it can be integrated into an existing pipeline and can restrict the following stage operation. Another argument for this concept is that the ALU has not to be used for the comparison, which makes it basically free for working on other tasks.

3.1.4.   Register Extension

Each piece of data, like constant values and addresses, has to be loaded into registers. The bounds should also be loaded into registers, so they can be used directly by the hardware comparators. This means that both kinds of data should be accessible from registers at the same time. The initially proposed register extension is shown in Figure 3-1.

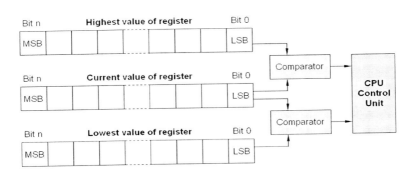

Figure 3-1: Register with Bound Storage

Modern processors include a wide number of registers and provide enough memory for both, values and associated bounds. Therefore, special bound registers can be added. An addressing scheme that guarantees the loading of corresponding bounds is rather complicated. Value and bounds would have to be stored with a certain offset to each other. Otherwise more information that gives advice about the memory position would have to be stored with the value and an additional calculation would cost a lot of performance. The more registers exist, the less re-loading is necessary. So, data can rest longer in memory and when it is needed again, re-loading is not required. If using normal registers for values and bounds, each newly loaded value with its corresponding bounds would consume space of three registers. In that case reloading does not take the time of one loading operation. It takes the time of three loading operations, two more for loading low and high bounds. Therefore, the operation of reloading costs more time and should be used as seldom as possible.

Another argument for the addition of special bound registers is based on architectural reasons. Bound registers must be linked to the comparator and not to the ALU as normal registers. If only one kind of registers exists, its architecture would require more hardware. Each register would have to include two multiplexers for reading and writing. These would have to manage from which input the register should accept and store data, as well as to which output the register data should be passed. Equivalent measures would have to be taken to adapt register files for different inputs and outputs.

Therefore, the addition of special bound registers for each existing register in the processor core seemed to be required. Bound registers have defined input and output sources and they are linked to the data-in port from the memory on one side and to the comparator on the other side. For corresponding bounds, the same register address is used. Since both types of registers are divided no problem of ambiguity arises. The number of registers for normal use can be kept. The amount of additional hardware is held as little as possible.

3.1.5. Instruction Set Extension

A change in software has to be expected, if the bounds should be loaded from memory into the registers. In this case, loading of bound data into bound registers must be realised. This can be done in two different ways, in either way an extension of the Instruction Set Architecture (ISA) is necessary.

The first concept leaves the loading operation as it is. Data continues to be loaded from memory into normal registers. This second approach leaves the architecture nearly unchanged, except the load-store procedure is modified. There exist exactly two instructions which may access the memory. The bounds should be stored in special bound registers. To transfer the data from normal to special registers a special move instruction *Move (MOV)* must be included. This instruction gets two operands specifying register addresses. The addresses belong to two different types of registers. So, the whole procedure of loading bounds into bound registers takes the time of loading and moving data.

Problems arise when the processor should now differentiate the kind of data moved from one register to a bounds register. At this low level the processor itself is not able to find out, if the data in a register is a bound or a value. This decision must be taken at a higher level. It is the compilers job to include transfer instructions at the proper positions. Therefore, the compiler is responsible for a better or worse performance. Concluding, if the code is highly optimised, the program will be fast. Otherwise each special *MOV* is preceded by a instruction *Load (LD)*, which happens to be slower than the execution of a single *LD* instruction.

While residing in intermediate registers, the bounds are not protected of being changed. Additional mechanisms would be necessary to secure this measure. Besides of securing a security measure not making sense, this approach is far away from the original concept. As many work as possible should be done by the hardware, because fewer changes in software result in higher security and acceptance of the new concept.

That is because low-level and hardware concepts in particular are more difficult to be circumvented by attackers. Furthermore, a technology that should be accepted by the market must not require big changes to previous systems. If using a normal register as intermediate storage position, there would be one register to be freed in the meanwhile. The freeing and storing of information takes a lot of time. The slower memory cannot react as fast as the registers in the processor. These operations consume time and the use should be economised. Therefore, another concept is proposed. Instead of adding special *MOV* instructions the procedure of loading was analyzed.

The bound registers could be explicitly filled by the use of special load instructions. These instructions would directly write bounds from memory to the bound registers. The advantage is that only one instruction per bound has to be executed. Moving is not necessary anymore, because the load procedure itself transfers the bound to the right destination.

The disadvantage is that the compiler has less flexibility to optimise the given code. The bounds have to be loaded directly before the value. So, the execution order is rather strict. At the same time it is an advantage to move responsibility from software to hardware level. Concluding, the hardware based solution results in better performance and security, when compared to other existing approaches.

3.2. Secure Bound Storage

An important aspect of bound checking in hardware is the way of storing additional bound information. Firstly, it is necessary to define, which data types have associated bounds and how these bounds look like. Secondly, the bound information, if available, has to be stored somewhere in hardware. In more detail this means that it is necessary to change the memory model of the used processor to add space for any existing bounds. Finally, it seems to be useful to add a protection mechanism to secure the usage of bounds.

3.2.1. Bound Information

It is necessary to define where the usage of bound information is useful and which should be stored. Depending on the available data types and how much these types could benefit from bound checking, it seems logically that data types, which represent references to other objects are mostly affected. The best examples for that are arrays. To each array a pointer is associated, which points to the first element of the array. When accessing an element, a copy of the pointer is taken and the position of the element is added to it. The calculated pointer is finally used to access the required element. The major problem is that it is possible to access storage locations which are outside of the defined array. A sample code for an illegal array access is shown Figure 3-2.

```
int i;
int array[6] = {1, 2, 3, 4, 5, 6};

for(i = 0; i < 10; i++) {
    array[i] = 1000;
}
```

Figure 3-2: Illegal Array Access

In the given sample, the program will write the last four values outside the array to storage locations, which could be used. To avoid this, it seems useful to associate bounds to the array. Figure 3-3 illustrates the comparison of array accesses without and with associated bounds.

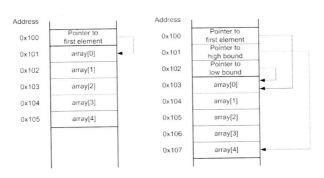

Figure 3-3: Comparison of Arrays without and with Bounds

45

The pointers to the first and last element of an array appear useful, because it is not possible anymore to access elements outside the array. In general, bounds for a data type, which represent a reference to another object, are the highest and the lowest addresses of the referenced object.

The same consideration could be done for primitive data types (e.g. an integer). The major difference to reference data types is that instead of addresses, data values are assigned as bounds. For a signed integer (length of four byte) the value -2147483648 (0x80000000) is set as low bound and the value 2147483647 (0x7FFFFFFF) is set as high bound. In case of an unsigned integer it would be 0 (0x00000000) and 4294967295 (0xFFFFFFFF).

Storing bound information for primitive data types is only legitimated, if sub range typing ranging is used. Sub range typing describes the partition of a data type into a smaller range. An example of such a sub range typing would be an integer, which is only defined from -6000 to 80000. In that particular example, bounds from -6000 (0xFFFFE890) to 80000 (0x00013880) would be useful, to check if the stored value is within this range. In all other cases, when using primitive types, storing bound information do not make sense, because the value of such a primitive data type can never be out of range.

Bounds are also useful for stack handling. Therefore, it is necessary to add low and high bound entries to each corresponding stack entry. For static storage, parameters and local variables on the stack the bounds would look like the same as described above. In case of return address, dynamic and static links (e.g. the saved FP) the situation is different. Especially these entries benefit from the additionally stored bound information. The reason for that is the possibility to check, if these entries are being changed. To establish this, low and high bound of a return address or a saved FP must be same as the return address or the saved FP. So, an attack (e.g. stack-smashing) to change those fields is not possible anymore and can easily be avoided.

A disadvantage of using bounds for entries like the return address, dynamic link or static link is that low and high bounds are always equal. On the one hand, there is a waste of memory and it would be enough to store only one copy of such an entry. On the other hand it seems to be useful to use bound checking, which is in any case implemented to check these entries too. Concluding, no other concept has to be implemented, because this is able to secure all stack entries.

3.2.2.   Memory Model without Paging

To save bounds in hardware, the memory model of the processor has to be changed in a way that additional information could be stored. So far, code and data are stored linear at beginning of specified addresses. This means that at a particular entry point the code segment of a program is placed and following to this the data segment. The space consumption of code and data segment is varying.

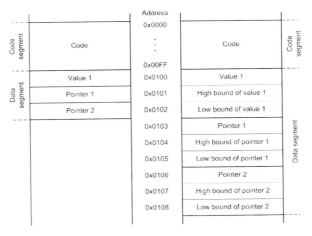

Figure 3-4: Memory Model without and with Bounds

As example the code segment reaches from 0x0000 to 0x00FF and the data segment reaches from 0x0100 to 0x0102. The discussed memory model is shown in the left of Figure 3-4.

To store additional bound information the data segment has to be extended, which is done by adding two additional storage entries after each existing. These locations represent low and high bounds of the corresponding entry. In detail, this modified memory model looks like the following: The code segment starts at an entry point 0x0000 and reaches until 0x00FF, afterwards the data segment is located. If the data segment consists of three variables, one primitive data type and two pointers, nine storage entries are needed. The additional entries are used to store the bound information of the objects in the data segment. To be able to assign a storage location for a low and a high bound to a corresponding data entry, it is necessary to group these elements. The first variable is located at address 0x0100 and the corresponding low and high bounds of this variable are located at address 0x0101 and 0x0102. Then the next variable or pointer and the associated bounds are placed. The modified memory model is shown in the right of Figure 3-4.

3.2.3. Memory Model with Paging

When using a Memory Management Unit (MMU), it seems to be useful to adapt the memory model too. The main reason is the circumstance that the memory is divided into pages of the same length. Grouping of data entries on one page and the corresponding low and high bounds on two other pages is possible. This model looks like the following: At the entry point the code segment is located. How many pages are needed is depending on the code and the page size. The data segment starts on the first completely free page after the code segment. The data entries will be placed on the first page of this segment. The next two pages will contain the low and high bounds of these entries on separate pages. If the original data segment – without bounds – will be larger than one page, the data entries are also split to more than one page. The effect for the new model is that after the existing pages, additional pages are located which are grouped in the same manner.

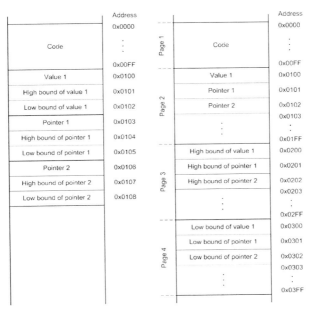

Figure 3-5: Memory Model without and with MMU

The model in the right of Figure 3-5 has several advantages: One is that the content of the data pages are the same as in conventional systems. This is shown by comparing the data segment in the left of Figure 3-4 with the second page entry in the right of Figure 3-5. The reason therefore is that low and high bounds are saved on different pages and they will not be merged into the data pages. Finally, this leads to an unchanged view on the memory from the programs side, because user programs will never see the pages, which contain the associated bounds. In cases of not fully filled pages, a waste of memory would appear. In general both models need three times memory for the data segments, but this is not preventable if a secure bound store should be established in hardware. Another problem could be the interoperability with existing operating systems, which have to be adopted for the introduced paging mechanism. Arrays were not considered in the paging mechanisms, because this depends on the MMU handling and architecture.

3.2.4.   Secure Usage of Bound Information

To implement a secure bound storage architecture, a change of the memory model was proposed. An important aspect is the insecurity of this additional bound information storage and usage. In the memory model, everybody is able to access the stored bound information, if the particular address is known. Another possible attack could be to overwrite the particular memory content. This shows that it is possible to change the stored bounds and to violate the bound checking mechanism. So, it is necessary to protect the bound information. A possible way is to mark each storage location, which contain bound information and to distinguish between data and associated bounds. When accessing a certain storage location the marking technique enables a check, if the particular access is allowed.

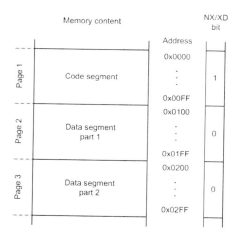

Figure 3-6: Memory Model with NX/XD bits

The developed concept is similar to the marking technique of AMD and Intel. They mark memory pages, which are non-executable by the help of NX and XD bits. The associated memory model is shown in Figure 3-6. [20, 21] It is necessary to modify this implementations to add the needed prevention techniques. The idea is to extend the field, which stores the security information from one to two bits.

Therefore, not only code and data – executable/non executable – could be distinguished, moreover two additional states – low bound and high bound – could be added. This modified field, which provides the needed security information, is called SecureTag. The possible states of the SecureTag are shown in Figure 3-7.

Type	Executable	Content	SecureTag
Code	Yes	Binary	11
Data	No	Value or address	00
Low bound	No	Value or address	01
High bound	No	Value or address	10

Figure 3-7: States of SecureTag

How the SecureTag is stored is depending on the used memory model and whether paging is used or not. If paging is not used, there has to be a corresponding two bit field for each storage location in memory where the SecureTag is stored. So, an additional data structure is needed. The memory model including the SecureTag and not using paging is shown in Figure 3-8.

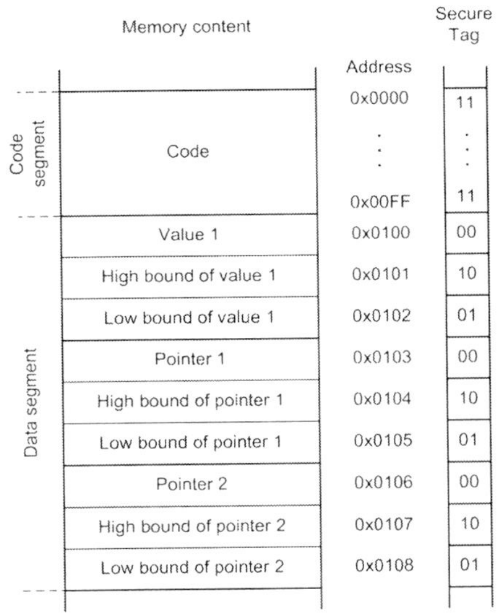

Figure 3-8: Memory Model with SecureTag

When using paging, the SecureTag could be added to the page table, as AMD and Intel have done it with their implementations. A separate data structure would also be possible, but the implementation in the page tables seems useful here. The memory model with paging is shown in Figure 3-9.

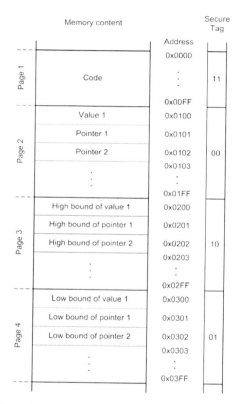

Figure 3-9: Memory Model with SecureTag and Paging

Concluding, the SecureTag concept can be used to mark memory lines with several states. Therefore, a selection between code, data, low and high bound can be done. It is relevant that this concept can be used in all memory and processor architectures. The limitation is in the operating system and software environment, which has to support the SecureTag technique.

3.3. Secure Exception Handling

A processor has to provide methods to handle errors, exceptions and unpredictable events. These events can appear due to the fact that errors occur during read or write instructions or that a Co-Processor (CP) or a Floating-Point Unit (FPU) indicates an exceptional condition or that external hardware interrupts are released. Such methods can be called traps.

It was decided to reconstruct the already existing trap handler to react to a detected buffer under/overflow. For that purpose a new trap type has to be implemented.

3.3.1. Trap handling

The handling of a trap has to be done in the following manner: Firstly, the operating system has to be changed from user to supervisor mode, provided that the existing user mode is preserved. By the means of the Current Window Pointer (CWP), which is located in the PSR, the register window is shifted to a new window. The first two local registers of the new window are used to store the current and the Next Program Counter (NPC). So, the operating system is enabled to return after the trap was treated. Finally, the trap handler address has to be calculated and transferred to the PC. If the exception is a reset trap, the control is transferred to the start address of the operating system.

3.3.2. Trap address generation

In a trap based exception handling environment, it is important, how the trap address generation is treated. Basically, there exist two ways of trap address calculation and generation: The first and more secure way is to use a static trap address, which is calculated by the processor, in case a buffer under/overflow is detected. Therefore, a bit mask of the induced exception is defined once. At this address the trap handler is located. It represents a piece of code, which guarantees the treatment of the trap.

The second way is to use a dynamic trap address, which depends on the implementation of the software exception model. It represents a try-catch programming language construct, shown in Figure 3-10, designed to handle the occurrence of a condition that changes the normal flow of execution.

```
try {
        ...
        // Code in which exceptions may occur
        ...
}
catch (OutOfBoundException e) {
        ...
        // Code to handle detected out-of-bounds exceptions
        ...
}
```

Figure 3-10: Software Try-Catch Block

To respond to a detected buffer overflow, the memory address of the catch block has to be passed to the processor before the trap occurs. This is done by the operating system by using the local registers of the new register window. In comparison to a static trap address the dynamic version allows the execution of user specific commands, which are located within the software catch block. The disadvantage can be a higher vulnerability, concerning the user specific code, located in the catch block.

3.3.3. Trap categories

An exception can cause any of three categories of traps: A precise trap is induced by an instruction during its execution and before any visible states of the program has been changed. The last instruction before the trap activation has to be executed and all following instructions will be ignored. A deferred trap is also induced by a particular command. Contrary to a precise trap, the deferred may occur after any program visible states have been changed. Such changes can be done by the execution of either the trap inducing instruction itself, or by one or more instructions following on that. A deferred trap occur one or more commands after the trap is induced. An interrupting trap is neither a precise nor a deferred trap. It is either an external interrupt request or an exception that is not directly related to a previously executed command or an exception caused by such an instruction. [6]

4. Proof of Concept

Before the proposed approach was implemented in hardware, a proof of concept in a suitable simulator was necessary. In this chapter, several simulators were evaluated concerning usability and costs. Since the evaluations are discussed in detail, the final conclusions are discussed in section 4.1.4. The implemented secure simulator extensions and the performance results are described in sections 4.4 and 4.5.

4.1. Evaluation of Simulators

When trying to find an optimal basis for a secure processor simulator, first general requirements were defined. It was important, to find a product, which would allow access to its source code. Since the creation of a new kind of Central Processing Unit (CPU) was intended, the CPU model should be interchangeable and self definable. Even the addition of registers and other components should be possible. Since there exist many different types, it was decided to pick out only the suitable ones. They will be introduced in the next sections, including their advantages and disadvantages.

4.1.1. von-Neumann Simulator

The von-Neumann simulator, which was published in [31], was written in Java and its main target is to give students a better understanding of the von-Neumann approach. Though its purpose is being a tool used in education and as the name suggests, its commands are based on the von-Neumann architecture. Since commands and microinstructions are predefined in code, they cannot be altered at runtime. Also the hardware structure is not interchangeable. The number of registers and memory are set according to a simple von-Neumann based CPU and a predefined fetch sequence with respect to the architecture is implemented. The fact of writing assembler programs and the necessary memory association (code versus data) is shown in Figure 4-1. Although there are two windows – one for the commands and one for the data – where the memory can be filled, both windows show the same memory location.

The only difference is the content representation. A line of code in program memory consists of an instruction and operands, a *0* is represented as *LOAD 0*. The according machine code is *0*, because *LOAD* has the Op-Code *000*. In the data window it works vice versa. So *LOAD 1* is simply represented as *1*.

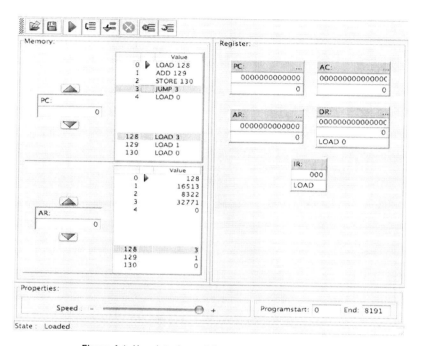

Figure 4-1: User interface of the von-Neumann simulator

All these predefined settings make this simulator simple to maintain and it would be a good choice. Since a completely new architecture should be defined, a dynamic change of machine components have to be possible and when a register in the architecture is changed, a recompilation must not be required. Concluding, this simulator is used for teaching to understand the von-Neumann architecture. A modular simulator is required for a scientific approach and so this tool can not be used for the simulation.

4.1.2. MikroSim

MikroSim was initially published in [32] and written in Pascal by H. Gasiorowski. Over the years the program was improved and a new concept was necessary. The new Version was written in Visual Basic by M. Perner in 1992. From that time the simulator transitioned according to changes in a lecture at Ludwig-Maximilians University in Munich and Philipps-University in Marburg. The developers of this simulator established a learning model, which will be introduced in the following paragraphs.

At the first step of the learning model there are just three visible components: Registers, busses and an ALU, which are connected to each other. The second layer provides a simple Random Access Memory (RAM), which includes MAR and MDR and two registers defining *Mode* and *Format* settings of the component. Furthermore, the content of the RAM can be filled externally by use of an editor. At the third layer, two new components are included: The microcode Read-Only Memory (ROM), which is defined in the processor's firmware and holds the microinstructions. As the RAM, the ROM can be externally filled by use of an editor. Since address resolution in ROM gets very tricky, when handling direct and indirect jumps, the processor has an associated ROM to solve these issues.

At the fourth and final layer the assembly language can be defined. Each machine instruction (assembly command) is defined by micro programs in ROM. The rather complex graphical user interface is shown in Figure 4-2. An op-code must be associated to each instruction. This part is realised in a very realistic manner. The op-code multiplied by four defines the location in ROM, where the micro program is located. Assembler programs are located in RAM, where each assembler command is processed by the execution of the associated micro program in ROM. An interpreter is located at the beginning of the ROM. It simply implements the load-increment-execute sequence. For a proper functionality certain invariants must be considered: At the beginning of each sequence the program counter must be incremented. Each micro program (assembler command) must return to the beginning of the sequence. Otherwise the machine stops.

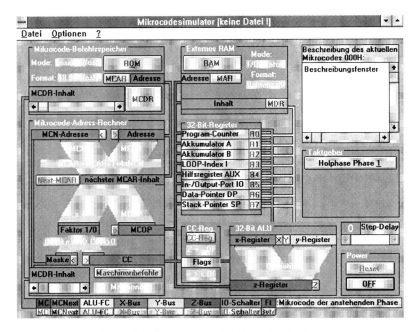

Figure 4-2: Graphical user interface of MikroSim

MikroSim is a very good tool for understanding a processor step by step in several layers, but due to the high costs and the complex design it is not suitable for the development of a secure CPU architecture.

4.1.3. CPUSim

CPUSim was developed by D. Skrien at Colby College in Waterville. Associated information was published in [33]. The simulator is based on the ideas in the STARTLE simulator developed by J.M. Kerridge of the Department of Computer Science, University of Sheffield in England. Its main focus is modelling CPUs at register-transfer level. A screenshot of the full graphical user interface is shown in Figure 4-3.

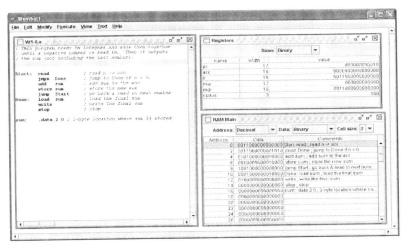

Figure 4-3: Graphical user interface of CPUSim

To design a CPU from the scratch, a selection of components is required. The CPU layout is created as a collection of hardware modules: registers, register arrays, RAMs and condition bits. The bit-width of each component can be selected freely. The RAMs are addressed by 8 bit values, so only the length can be chosen. For providing greater widths, the same approach as for the x86 processor, was selected. For a width of 16 bit per address a double-increment have to be implemented that the bytes can be defined as least and most significant. Register arrays seem to be useful when implementing register based machines. The advantage is that a large number of registers can be approached by a smaller number of index registers. As a result, for a register array with four entries only two register indices are required. From a mathematical point of view, the square root of the number of entries defines the number of index registers. When working pseudo parallel with many registers of the array, one index register per entry, has to be provided. In each machine design at least one condition bit – the halt bit – has to be provided that stops the machine, when it is set. For each condition bit a register or a part of it has to be used. The hardware modules dialog is shown in Figure 4-4.

Figure 4-4: Hardware modules dialog

When all hardware modules have been selected, microinstruction definitions have to be accomplished. In CPUSim the microinstructions are split up into 14 categories. The associated dialog is shown in Figure 4-5

Figure 4-5: Microinstruction dialog

Since a CPU is made of individual components, connections must be defined. Transfer microinstructions had to be used to connect the components and enables information transfer. To define these instructions, two parameters (source and destination) have to be provided. Furthermore, the start bit and number of bits that should be transferred must be specified. When defining a register-to-register array connection additional information about the indexing is needed. In CPUSim functionalities provided by hardware modules are defined as microinstructions. An ALU cannot be defined and so its functionality resides in the microinstruction category, where also mathematical operations have to be defined. For each operand a register has to be provided, as well as a destination register and optional registers for overflow and carry can be specified. The simulator can process arithmetic operations as addition, subtraction, multiplication and division.

The decode microinstruction is hard-coded. Therefore, only one instruction register, where the instruction should be decoded, can be chosen. Further important microinstructions are increment and memory access. As proposed before, the increment delta can be specified freely. This is necessary to be able to approach two bytes of memory at once. The step size must be provided in bytes, because one cell in memory has eight bits. The memory can transfer information into both directions. Two registers, which provide source/destination and address, must be specified. When writing, the value of a source register is written to the address in memory, which is the current value of the address register. Reading is done the other way round. A useful feature of CPUSim is that the source/destination register can vary between read and write operation. Moreover, microinstructions dealing with binary operators and executing jumps to another line of code exist. For further information see the CPU Manual, published in [33].

When all microinstructions were successfully defined, the next step in CPU design – the definition of machine instructions – can be accomplished. A machine instruction is made of a sequence of microinstructions. For better usability the instruction dialog, which is shown in Figure 4-6, was divided into three columns. The first one holds a list of already defined instructions. In this table an op-code and parameter lengths for the instruction can be determined. The op-code is used by the control unit. When an instruction was chosen, its microcode is shown in the second column. The code is implemented by dragging and dropping microinstructions from the third column and bringing them into the right order. The microinstructions are shown in a tree structure, in which nodes symbolise the categories, as well as leafs symbolise the microinstruction names. At the bottom of the tree a not self defined system microinstruction, named *End*, is located.

This microinstruction has to be the last microinstruction in each instruction. It returns the authority to the fetch-sequence, which is thereby instructed to fetch the next instruction from the memory.

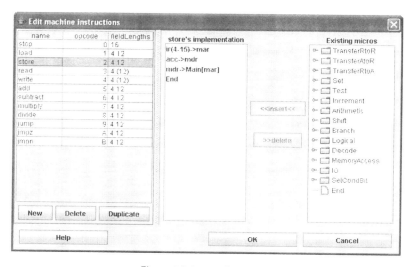

Figure 4-6: Instruction dialog

This so-called fetch sequence defines the order of the dataflow from memory through the different registers up to the instruction register. In CPUSim this sequence is implemented by *Transfer* microinstructions, transferring data to the instruction register. However, the fetch sequence has to fulfil more tasks. It is responsible for the increment of the program counter, as soon as the data from memory has arrived in the instruction register and it has to decode the op-code from the address. The op-code is passed to the control unit, and the address gives the parameters of the instruction.

With the definition of the fetch sequence the hardware and firmware are ready to go. So the self-designed CPU can be tested. This is done by implementation and execution of assembler programs. For this job, CPUSim provides a special editor. The *.data* pseudo-instruction enables the memory allocation for a variable, is. Its width is given in bytes and the variable can be used in the program providing its label. Like other source codes, such an assembler program has to be assembled and loaded to memory. It is important that the first instruction is located at position 0 in the memory, because the fetch-sequence starts fetching at 0.

For debugging the assembler programs, a special debug mode was implemented in CPUSim. It supports several steps of execution. When *Step by Instr* was chosen, the programmer is not hindered by the fetch-sequence internals. The instructions are executed at once and only the instruction result is shown. When thinking the bug could be going out from a failure in microinstruction implementation, *Step by Micro* should be chosen. In this mode the simulator steps inside of each instruction. A useful debugging feature is that the last instruction can be back upped. The debug toolbar is shown in Figure 4-7.

Figure 4-7: Debug toolbar

4.1.4.   Conclusion

The von-Neumann simulator, discussed in section 4.1.1, could not be used, because a completely new architecture has to be defined and a dynamic interchange of machine components is necessary.

MikroSim, described in section 4.1.2, is a very good tool for understanding a processor step by step in several layers, but due to the high costs and the complex design it is not suitable for the usage in the Secure CPU project.

Regarding the extensibility and possibility to interchange several parts of the simulator engine, CPUSim was selected for building up the secure CPU architecture. Furthermore, the source code is available for free and can be extended easily by the use of the common programming language Java. The selected simulator was discussed in detail in section 4.1.3.

4.2. Design Patterns in CPUSim

In software technology design patterns represent predefined solutions to functionality, which are frequently required in software projects. Hardly each problem can be solved by use of an already existing pattern. So, problems that were already processed by creating a pattern must not be taken into account anymore. A software developer can concentrate on the essential of his program solving default problems by the use of predefined design patterns.

4.2.1. Prototyping

When creating many modules of similar types, *prototyping* turns out to be useful. Prototyping means creation of an object, that is a complete instance of a class, but that was defined with default parameters only. At runtime new microinstructions can be defined in CPUSim. The user specifies new parameters, completing the module configuration. By use of the new configuration the pre-defined prototype is cloned and the new module can be instantiated according to the new parameters.

4.2.2. Factory

A factory does the pre-creation of such a prototype. Factories are widely used in Java programs. The later used module configuration is done in the factory. So that modules are only instantiated when previously configured. Otherwise only the prototype exists until the configuration is done.

In CPUSim the factories specify the graphical representation of modules. Since there exist many similar types of modules, the graphical user interface uses tables. These interactive tables allow the user to configure the module's parameters. Therefore, *cellEditors* and *cellRenderers* are defined for each cell. Although the intelligent JavaBeans system defines defaults, sometimes according *cellEditors* or cell*Renderers* must be defined manually. Furthermore, the column titles are defined in the factory. The order is defined by the order of the String array and though the number of arrays must be equal to the number of defined JavaBeans.

4.2.3.   JavaBeans

JavaBeans integrate component technology to the Java platform. With the JavaBeans Application Programming Interface (API) reusable, platform-independent components can be created. Using JavaBeans-compliant application builder tools, these components can also be integrated into applets, applications, or composite components. In CPUSim each module is represented as JavaBean. This means that there exists a member with the JavaBean name and a setter and getter function for it. These three items are required by the JavaBeans API, which provides consistent access to member variables. Since JavaBeans are a standardisation, they require function names to follow strict rules. These include Java-style naming and case-sensitivity. The only difficulty in using JavaBeans is the unavailability of error messages. In case of a badly defined JavaBean, the error turns out during accessing.

4.3.   Handling of CPUSim

This section deals with the instruction execution and the error handling of CPUSim. Furthermore, the *MachineWriter* and *MachineReader* functionality is roughly explained.

4.3.1.   Instruction execution

At assembling time, each instruction is broken down to its microinstructions. The assembled program is then represented as a big vector of microinstructions. When the machine is executed a loop over the whole vector is started. During simulation the control unit keeps track of the micro program that is executed. This becomes important when a program or machine is to be debugged.

The execution is done in particular threads, though the graphical user interface stays responsive in the meantime. There are different modes that require special exceptions to be fired. Apart from error exceptions, the execution is built around events that implement debugger functionality and count ability of cycles. Errors are thrown when the current micro index gets out of range. This functionality is used for execution abortion. To make the machine halt the execution of the last microinstructions in a micro program must only be skipped. This means that some of them are omitted and the current microinstruction points to an *End* or *Out of range* microinstruction. This can be used for abortion when a microinstruction leads to a negative result. A useful extension would be an interrupt handling, which would not require the machine to restart each time an exception was thrown.

The debugging toolbar allows the user to specify an execution step size and one of three modes: Either the program is executed up to the next break point, or the debugger breaks after each instruction or microinstruction. This variable step size is implemented by exceptions, which are fired after each successfully executed step. A special exception is fired when the control unit recognises that a new fetch instruction has to be executed. Since the fetch-cycle is defined by means of microinstructions the machine only needs to watch for an instruction with the associated type *Fetch-sequence*.

4.3.2. MachineWriter and MachineReader

In CPUSim, machines can be stored in extensible Markup Language (XML) or HyperText Markup Language (HTML) format. At the moment XML is used to save the core. HTML is just used for documentation purposes. The generated HTML files describe the machine contents in a concise way. Machine instructions, microinstruction and hardware components are represented in tables. For creating valid XML files, the Document Type Definition (DTD) is written before the content. The DTD defines a grammar, which rules each CPU File has to follow and the content is tested against that grammar when reading. Therefore, the DTD must exist and has to be provided to a parser. The CPU-File content consists of tags defining hardware modules, microinstructions and instructions. Furthermore, it describes the special instruction fetch-sequence by a number of microinstructions. The *MachineWriter* applies a distinct barcode to hardware modules and microinstructions.

A previously written machine is read in a 3-step-procedure. The XML file is pre-processed by the LAX parser, which prepares the data and considers special features of CPUSim. This has to be done in the pre-processor because the SAX parser is a commercial XML tool. For that sources were not available for the developers. The SAX parser finally gets the prepared XML file and parses it, as well as checks it against the DTD. The validated structure is finally returned to the *MachineReader*, which recreates the stored machine. For that purpose the new machine with all its microinstructions, instructions and hardware modules has to be instantiated. During this recreational process, the input data is checked. These tests include checks against data types and meaningful numbers.

4.3.3. Error handling

Errors, which occur during the parsing procedure, are transmitted directly to CPUSim. Exceptions are thrown from the SAX parser and, when not caught, thrown to the execution unit in CPUSim. This execution unit reacts and throws an error message and as a result debugging of old CPU-Files gets hard.

4.4. Design of Simulator

For the simulation a secure architecture, three different features were implemented: A cycle counter, which is necessary to measure the performance, as well as a register extension and a memory marking technique using the SecureTag.

4.4.1. Cycle Counter

A common problem in simulations is the revision of results to the real world. Fundamentally, simulation time of a designed machine in CPUSim cannot be compared to time consumed for an instruction to get executed in hardware. To get around this problem a counter utility was implemented. The utility consists of three independent counters, which consider machine cycles, microinstructions per machine instruction and total number of microinstructions. By the result of the counters, assembler programs can be compared to each other with respect to performance. The results can easily be revised to a real hardware CPU. Therefore, the counter values are simply multiplied by the mean value of time the machine needs to execute such an operation. Since the counters are only incrementing by discrete steps, the simulated results are independent from the time consumed in the simulator.

In CPUSim the machine execution is realised as a loop over all microinstructions. Though, an implementation of a counter is easy, because in each loop the micro counter is incremented. This counts the total number of microinstructions that have been executed. For the trickier problem of counting the microinstructions per unit, the micro index can be used. It is incremented after each microinstruction execution. Since the necessary functionality for the microinstructions to be counted already existed no special counter mechanism had to be implemented. The cycle counter makes use of the already implemented *RUN_AND_FIRE_CYCLES* execution mode. Every time the instruction type equals the special instruction *Fetch-sequence*, an event telling what happened, is fired. Since the instruction type is already usefully checked, the counter must only be incremented each time the check returns true. The *RUN_AND_FIRE_CYCLES* was only used in some run modes, following the other call modes had to be adapted.

The most difficult functionality, which had to be implemented, is the reset mechanism. The initialisation values are set in the machine constructor, but the counters can be reset whenever the user wants. Though, counting of a part of the instructions can be done if needed. A second way to reset the counters is the *Reset Control Unit* button, which also sets the control unit back to its initial values. For keeping the user interface concisely, the counters and the new button *Reset Counters* were integrated into the debug toolbar, as shown in Figure 4-8.

Figure 4-8: New block appending the default debug toolbar

68

4.4.2. Direct Register Comparison

CPUSim implements the comparison of two register values only by the use of arithmetic operations. The existing *Test* microinstruction allows comparing a register value to an arbitrary value. An arithmetic microinstruction can subtract two registers. To be able to test the intermediate result, it has to be stored into an additional register. Then, it is compared to the arbitrary value. If the result is positive, the next microinstruction is executed. Otherwise delta microinstructions are omitted. The omission must be chosen in a way, which guarantees that the following microinstruction points to an *End* microinstruction or a microinstruction which index is *out of range*. Such a procedure takes very long with respect to its functionality. In hardware a single comparator could achieve the same functionality in less time.

With respect to this case, the time consumed in the simulator could not be revised to the real world. To make the performance measurements better revisable the *Test* microinstruction was adapted to these needs, as shown in Figure 4-9.

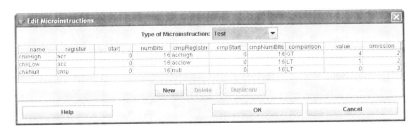

Figure 4-9: New microinstruction dialog

Instead of a *cellEditor*, where the arbitrary value could be given, a *cellRenderer* showing all existing registers in a combo box was implemented. A *cmpRegister* can be chosen, which will be directly compared to another register. The start bit and number of bits taken from the register can also be specified. This enables to check registers against different lengths of values. For the addition of columns into an existing microinstruction a new JavaBean has to be created in the microinstruction type class. A column specifier has to be added to the

69

properties string of the microinstruction type factory. Next, the type constructor has to be adapted according to the new parameters.

By now the new or adapted module can be used in any machine design. What was taken apart until now is the ability to store and load machines. To allow this feature the *getHTMLDescription* and *getXMLDescription* have to be adapted. These functions are called whenever the microinstructions have to written to a file. For making written files readable for the *MachineReader* the DTD in the *MachineWriter* must be adjusted. The last step is to adapt the microinstruction type start method in the *MachineReader*. According to the given requirements, the *MachineWriter* had to be modified too.

4.4.3.   Memory Marking via SecureTag

In the original package for defining a memory, it is necessary to specify a name and a length. If a length of 128 is provided, CPUSim creates a memory divided in 128 addresses and to each address one byte is assigned. In addition there is now the possibly to specify the width of the memory, which is specified in bytes. If a memory of length 128 and width 2 is defined, CPUSim creates a memory, which has also 128 addresses. The difference is that to each address two bytes assigned, so there are 256 bytes total. The possible settings of width are between one and eight bytes. The reason for not allowing more than eight bytes is that it would not make sense. This is mainly caused by the circumstance that a register or register array could not be defined to values grater than 64 bits. Another reason is that the handling of more than eight byte in Java – but not only in Java – is not easy, because the greatest data type is a long (eight byte), handling of more than eight byte as memory length is complex and not supported in CPUSim.

After this implementation the implementation of an extension of NX/XD bit – called SecureTag could be done. By the help of this tag, it is possible to divide the RAM into more than two parts as only code and data. Furthermore, hardware based bounds checking can be added to the processor core. To implement the SecureTag, it was necessary to add new microinstructions, which handle the tag. Instructions for transferring tags from memory to a register and in the other direction were needed. Moreover other instructions for setting and testing the tag had to be implemented. This is mainly caused by the reason that tags are often set to defined values, respectively compared with those. In addition, this reduces the number of needed microinstructions in a single machine instruction. In CPUSim three microinstructions were added, which are shown in Figure 4-10. To distinguish between primitive data types and pointers in CPUSim assembler, it was necessary to add also a pseudo instruction called .ptr.

Name	SecureTag Access	Set SecureTag	Test SecureTag
Description	Move a tag from or to a register	Set a tag in memory	Compare a tag with a value
Direction	Memory Read/Write	-	-
Data	Determine register to read or write	Register that defines address	Value, which should be set
Address	Register that defines address	Value, which should be set	Register that defines address
Compare	-	-	Less, greater, equal, not equal
Omission	-	-	Number of micros

Figure 4-10: Micro instructions for SecureTag

To handle the SecureTag a fixed procedure has to be followed:

- Firstly, the tag has to be set, while loading code and data into the memory. Additionally the correct values for low and high bounds have to be set. In conventional systems this procedure is done by the operating system or the compiler, but in case of the secure CPUSim extension, it is done by the simulator.

- Secondly, the tag has to be read in each fetch cycle, before an instruction is decoded. This is to ensure that only code is executed.

- Thirdly, on write access to memory – writing of data values or pointer addresses – the tag and the associated bounds are loaded. Additionally the bounds of the affected data entry are checked, to ensure that the data value or pointer is valid.

- Finally, the tag has to be pushed onto or popped from the stack. In addition to the particular data, the associated bounds have to be pushed or popped too.

The CPUSim source code file *cpusim.module.RAM.java* contains the class, which implements a memory module. It provides methods for accessing the memory, changing the attributes (name, length, and width) of the memory, loading the assembled instructions into the memory and load/save the contents of the memory from/to a file. The new secure members (illustrated in bold) of the RAM class, as well as the existing ones are shown in Figure 4-11.

```
byte[] data;                    //contains data of memory
int length;                     //length of memory
int bytes;                      //width in bytes of memory
boolean[] breaks;               //set breaks for debugging
String[] comments;              //contains comments to data
boolean haltAtBreaks;           //Halt at breaks enable
byte[] secureTags;              //contains SecureTags
int numBytesForSecureTags;      //needed bytes for all tags
```

Figure 4-11: Members of RAM class

The structure for the memory data has not changed in comparison to the original implementation. The difference is that the byte array has now a length of length*bytes instead of length. So, if a memory module of length 12 and width 2 is defined, a byte array of length 24 will be created.

A byte array was chosen, as a suitable data structure for the SecureTags. The length of this array depends of the circumstance, how many tags are fitting into one byte. The width of the tag is changeable by the constant *NUM_SECURE_TAGS_IN_BYTE* defined in the file *cpusim.util.CPUSim-Constants.java*. The possible settings of this constant are 1, 2, 4 and 8. In the current implementation, these constant is set to two, which means that to each address a 2 bit SecureTag is associated. The dynamic member *numBytesForSecureTags* contains the number of bytes needed for all SecureTags. Furthermore, another file *cpusim.assembler.Assembled-*

InstructionCall.java contains the class, which implements the representation of an assembled instruction. The secure members (illustrated in bold), as well as the existing instruction call class members are shown in Figure 4-12.

```
int numBytes;                    // Total size of bytes in instruction call
byte instrType;                  // 0: data, 1: low bound, 2: high bound, 3: code
boolean isFirstDataEntry;        // True if instruction contains the first bytes of data
int dataOperandsCellSize;        // Cell size of an operand in pseudo instruction
int dataNumOperands;             // Number of operands in pseudo instruction
long value;                      // Value of this instruction call
String comment;                  // Comment for instruction call
```

Figure 4-12: Members of instruction call class

The instruction type is necessary, while loading the code into the memory. This type decides which value of the SecureTag should be set. The boolean member *isFirstDataEntry* is needed, because it is possible to define storage locations, which are greater than eight bytes. In such cases the instruction is divided into more than one instruction – an instruction could not contain values greater than a long – and the first part is marked to sign the beginning. The members *dataNumOperands* and *dataOperandsCellSize* are needed while calculating the bounds of a pseudo instruction. It is necessary to know the number of operands and the length of those. The existing methods of this class are adapted to the new structure. The package *cpusim.microinstruction.** contains all existing microinstructions of CPUSim.

4.4.4.   Structure of Simulated CPU

This simulation in CPUSim should demonstrate the usage of the SecureTag. Firstly the structure, which means registers, memories and condition bits, of the processor are created. Secondly, necessary microinstructions are defined. Next, these microinstructions are used to generate associated machine instructions. Finally, to test the functionality of the SecureTag, particular assembler files are written and extended. A screenshot of the modified and secured simulator CPUSim version 3.1.1 is shown in Figure 4-13.

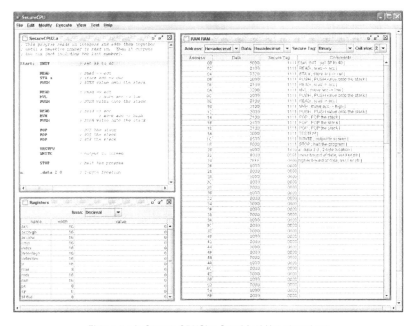

Figure 4-13: Secure CPUSim Graphical User Interface

In this simulation a 16 bit CPU with an op-code length of 8 bit is used. There is one memory with a length of 128 and a width of 2 bits. The simulated processor includes eight condition bits, which are set, if a certain event has occurred. The condition bits are shown in Figure 4-14.

Name	Register	Bit	Halt
halt-bit	Status	0	True
carry-bit	Status	1	False
data-executed-bit	Status	2	True
accessed-non-data-area-bit	Status	3	True
acc-lowbound-bit	Status	4	True
acc-highbound-bit	Status	5	True
index-lowbound-bit	Status	6	True
index-highbound-bit	Status	7	True

Figure 4-14: Condition bits

The registers, which were used in the simulated processor, are shown in Figure 4-15.

Name	Width	Description
acc	16	Accumulator
acchigh	16	High bound of accumulator
acclow	16	Low bound of accumulator
datalength	16	Number of addresses used by a storage location
index	16	Address of the storage location
indexhigh	16	High bound of the storage location
indexlow	16	Low bound of the storage location
ir	16	Instruction register
mar	8	Memory address register
mdr	16	Memory data register
null	16	Null register
pc	8	Program counter
sp	8	Stack pointer
status	8	Status register

Figure 4-15: Processor register

In addition to the halt and carry bits, which show a violation due to a buffer overflow condition were added. The data-executed bit is set, if a process tries to execute code in data regions. The accessed-non-data-area bit is set, if an accesses in read or write instructions non data regions occur. The low bound and high bound bits are set if a violation against a bound of accumulator or index register had happened.

4.4.5.   New Machine Instructions

For the usage of the SecureTag, as well as the memory marking and checking technique several new machine instructions were necessary. In the following the most important new machine instructions are listed in detail. The field lengths are always 8 bit op-code and 8 bit operand. The stack instructions do not need the operand, because the values are directly pushed from the accumulator onto the stack.

The *LDA* instruction loads the accumulator with a value from memory. Which entry from memory is chosen depends from the given operand that contains the address. The list of micro instructions including comments is shown in Figure 4-16.

Microinstructions	Comment
ir(8-15)->mar	Get operand
testRAMst[mar]=DATA|+1	Test SecureTag
set-accsessed-non-data-bit	Set condition bit
dec_mar	Search for start of data location
testRAMst[mar]=DATA|-2	Test SecureTag
inc_mar	Increment address register
clear_datalength	Set data length to 0
inc_datalength	Calculate data lentgh
inc_mar	Increment address register
testRAMst[mar]=DATA|-3	Test SecureTag
ir(8-15)->mar	Get operand
RAM[mar]->mdr	Get data from RAM
mdr->acc	Store data in accumulator
mar+datalength->mar	Set mar to low bound
RAM[mar]->mdr	Get data from RAM
mdr->acclow	Store data in low bound of accumulator
mar+datalength->mar	Set mar to high bound
RAM[mar]->mdr	Get data from RAM
mdr->acchigh	Store data in high bound of accumulator
End	End instruction

Figure 4-16: LDA machine instruction

The *LDPTR* instruction loads a pointer from memory into the index register. Which entry from memory is chosen depends from the given operand that contains the address. The list of micro instructions including comments is shown in Figure 4-17.

Microinstructions	Comment
ir(8-15)->mar	Get operand
testRAMst[mar]=DATA|+1	Test Secure-Tag
set-accsessed-non-data-bit	Set condition bit
RAM[mar]->mdr	Get pointer from memory
mdr->index	Store pointer to index register
End	End instruction

Figure 4-17: LDPTR machine instruction

The *STA* instruction stores the accumulator into the memory. Which entry from memory is chosen depends from the given operand – contains the address. The list of micro instructions including comments is shown in Figure 4-18.

Microinstructions	Comment
ir(8-15)->mar	Tet operand
testRAMst[mar]=DATA|+1	Test SecureTag
set-accsessed-non-data-bit	Set condition bit
dec_mar	search for beginning of data location
testRAMst[mar]=DATA|-2	Test SecureTag
inc_mar	Increment address register
clear_datalength	Set data length to 0
inc_datalength	Calculate data lentgh
inc_mar	Increment address register
testRAMst[mar]=DATA|-3	Test SecureTag
ir(8-15)->mar	Get operand
mar+datalength->mar	Set mar to low bound
RAM[mar]->mdr	Get data from RAM
mdr->acclow	Store data in low bound of accumulator
mar+datalength->mar	Set mar to high bound
RAM[mar]->mdr	Get data from RAM
mdr->acchigh	Store data in high bound of accumulator
chkAccLow	Check low bound
set-acc-lowbound-bit	Set condition bit
chkAccHigh	Check high bound
set-acc-highbound-bit	Set condition bit
ir(8-15)->mar	Get operand
acc->mdr	Store accumulator in MDR
mdr->RAM[mar]	Store data in RAM
End	End instruction

Figure 4-18: STA machine instruction

The STPTR instruction stores the pointer in index register into the memory. Which entry from memory is chosen depends from the given operand that contains the address. The list of micro instructions including comments is shown in Figure 4-19.

77

Microinstructions	Comment
ir(8-15)->mar	Get operand
testRAMst[mar]=DATA|+1	Test SecureTag
set-accsessed-non-data-bit	Set condition bit
dec_mar	Search bor beginning of pointer location
testRAMst[mar]=DATA|-2	Test SecureTag
inc_mar	Increment address register
clear_datalength	Set data length to 0
inc_datalength	Calculate data lentgh
inc_mar	Increment address register
testRAMst[mar]=DATA|-3	Test SecureTag
ir(8-15)->mar	Get operand
mar+datalength->mar	Set mar to low bound
RAM[mar]->mdr	Get data from RAM
mdr->indexlow	Store data in low bound of index register
mar+datalength->mar	Set mar to high bound
RAM[mar]->mdr	Get data from RAM
mdr->indexhigh	Store data in high bound of index register
chkIndexLow	Check low bound
set-index-lowbound-bit	Set condition bit
chkIndexHigh	Check high bound
set-index-highbound-bit	Set condition bit
ir(8-15)->mar	Get operand
index->mdr	Store index register in MDR
mdr->RAM[mar]	Store data in RAM
End	End instruction

Figure 4-19: STPTR machine instruction

The *PUSH* instruction pushes a value from accumulator with low and high bounds to the stack. The list of micro instructions is shown in Figure 4-20.

Microinstructions	Comment
acc->mdr	Store accumulator to MDR
mdr->RAM[sp]	Store data in RAM
setRAMst[sp]=DATA	Set SecureTag to DATA
inc_sp	Increment stack pointer
acclow->mdr	Store low bound of accumulator to MDR
mdr->RAM[sp]	Store data in RAM
setRAMst[sp]=LOWB	Set SecureTag to LOWBOUND
inc_sp	Increment stack pointer
acchigh->mdr	Store high bound of accumulator to MDR
mdr->RAM[sp]	Store data in RAM
setRAMst[sp]=HIGHB	Set SecureTag to HIGHBOUND
inc_sp	Increment stack pointer
End	End instruction

Figure 4-20: PUSH machine instruction

78

The *POP* instruction popes a value from stack to the accumulator. The list of micro instructions including comments is shown in Figure 4-21.

Microinstructions	Comment
dec_sp	Decrement stack pointer
RAM[sp]->mdr	Store data from RAM to MDR
mdr->acchigh	Store MDR to high bound of accumulator
clearRAMst[sp]	Set SecureTag to 0
dec_sp	Decrement stack pointer
RAM[sp]->mdr	Store data from RAM to MDR
mdr->acclow	Store MDR to low bound of accumulator
clearRAMst[sp]	Set SecureTag to 0
dec_sp	Decrement stack pointer
RAM[sp]->mdr	Store data from RAM to MDR
mdr->acc	Store MDR to accumulator
clearRAMst[sp]	Set SecureTag to 0
End	End instruction

Figure 4-21: POP machine instruction

4.4.6. Modified Fetch Sequence

In the fetch sequence, it is necessary to check before decoding a machine instruction, whether the current address points to a code region in memory. This is done by testing the SecureTag before decoding the instruction The microinstructions, which are included in the modified fetch sequence, are shown in Figure 4-22.

Microinstructions	Comments
pc->mar	Set MAR to program counter
RAM[mar]->mdr	Read data from MAR in MDR
mdr->ir	Store MDR in instruction register
inc_pc	Increment program counter
testRAMst[mar]=CODE|+1	Test SecureTag
set-data-executed-bit	Set data execute bit
decode	Decode instruction

Figure 4-22: Fetch sequence

4.5.   Results

Before the architecture could be implemented in hardware, the proposed design had to be verified with a simulator. The simulator implementation does not contain any compiler modifications and represents a proof of concept. The performance was evaluated by the use of the integrated counters, in which the counter is incremented for each executed microinstruction. The performance of the approach could be measured independent of time. So, the counter results can be related to a real hardware, when it is multiplied by the mean execution time of a target processor core.

To evaluate the performance influence, a short assembler program (shown in Figure 4-23) was created for CPUSim. The op-code *TESTxx* in line 06 represents for both test implementations, arithmetic (software based) and direct (firmware based).

```
01      READ                    ; Read to ACC
02      MVL                     ; Move ACC to ACCLOW
03      READ                    ; Read to ACC
04      MVH                     ; Move ACC to ACCHIGH
05      READ                    ; Read to ACC
06      TESTxx              ; Performs Bound Check
07      STOP                    ; Stop the machine
```

Figure 4-23: CPUSim Evaluation Code

To proof the concept, the test program simulated only a single bound check, because it is easier to evaluate the results. The results showed that the number of simulator cycles is the same, but the number of micro instructions for both checking techniques differs. Concluding, per bound check 2 additional micro instructions are needed, as shown in Figure 4-24.

	Direct	**Arithmetic**
Used op-code	TESTFW	TESTSW
Number of bound checks	1	1
Number of cycles	7	7
Number of micro instructions	49	51

Figure 4-24: CPUSim Evaluation Code Results

The RAM snapshot is shown in Figure 4-25. The status of associated SecureTags is shown, as well as the data values, as well as the bounds of the evaluation assembler program.

80

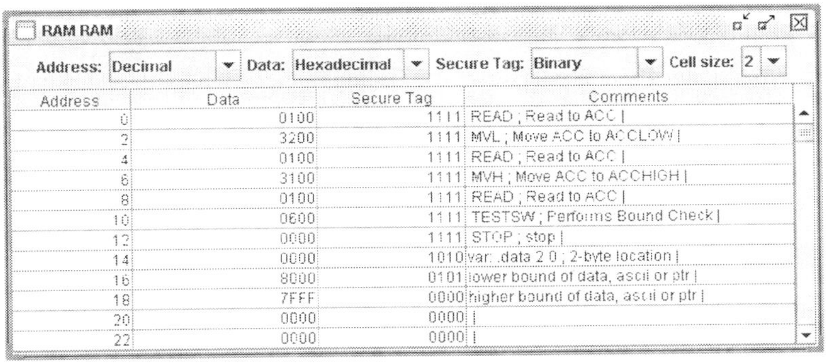

Figure 4-25: CPUSim RAM Snapshot

The counters result showed that direct comparison of registers resulted in a performance increase, when compared to an arithmetic comparison. Since the comparison was used excessively for the proposed bound checking design, a gap per bound check results in a high performance gain. The good results of our approach can be illustrated in more detail, when the number of bound checks is increased. Extrapolated values of bound checking operations are shown in Figure 4-26.

	Direct	Arithmetic
Number of bound checks	1000	1000
Number of additional micro instructions	2000	4000
Intermediate register necessary	No	Yes
Hardware modification necessary	Yes	No

Figure 4-26: CPUSim Performance Table

The direct approach needs less hardware utilization than the arithmetic, but the second needs two additional registers. First, the intermediate result has to be stored in a register. Afterwards, this result must be compared to a null register using the less than operation. Although some CPUs already include a null register, the arithmetic comparison requires an additional register in our adapted simulator. If more register bounds should be checked at the same time, the amount of additional registers increases. The illustration of the extrapolated results is shown in Figure 4-27.

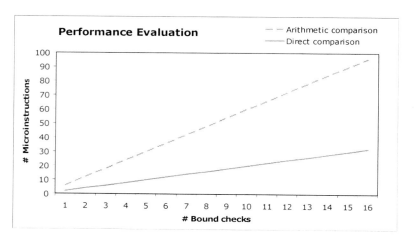

Figure 4-27: CPUSim Performance Chart

If an exception is thrown, which means an underflow or overflow happened, a pop-up dialog with the message *Execution Error* is shown. Considering the good results of the adapted processor, called Secure CPU, our implementation safes energy and increases security noticeable. The security advantage can be confirmed, because the SecureTag technique, as well as the direct register comparison provides a lower vulnerability, when compared to the former existing implementation.

5. System Configuration

This chapter contains the configuration of the LEON 2 processor core for different development boards. Firstly, the processor core configuration and the synthesis of the LEON 2 are discussed. Secondly, the specifications and synthesis processes of both considered development boards are described in detail. Finally, the selected software environment, including a rough overview of operating system and compilation chain is outlined.

5.1. Configuration of LEON 2

Before the synthesis of LEON 2 processor could be started, the processor has to be configured. For configuration and synthesis either a Linux platform or a Windows Cygwin platform is needed. The detailed requirements are published in [34].

There are two possibilities of configuring the LEON 2 processor. The first is to use any of the provided templates, which could be found at *leon2-1.0.32-xst/boards*. Gaisler Research provides scripts for configuring and synthesis for particular boards. For example:

- Gaisler/Pender GR-XC3S-1500 (Xilinx XC3S1500)

- XESS XSV800 prototype board (Xilinx XCV800)

By typing *make config* at the top-level directory the configuration for a particular board is done and saved to the VHDL configuration file *leon2-1.0.32-xst/leon/device.vhd*. This file is generated each time a configuration is accomplished. For targeting other boards it is necessary to add the *BOARD* switch in the command line. This switch is used to select a subdirectory of *leon2-1.0.32-xst/boards*. So for targeting for example the GR-XC3S-1500 board the command must be *make config BOARD=gr-xc3s1500*. Each subdirectory of *leon2-1.0.32-xst/boards* contains a default configuration file named *config-default* which is used per default. To use another configuration file the *CONFIG* switch has to be added to the command line too.

The main menu of the graphical configuration tool is divided in subcategories and by choosing one categories another window will be opened and the submenu for the selected subcategory appears, where the configuration settings can be changed. The working directory of the graphical configuration tool is *leon2-1.0.32-xst/tkconfig*. If the configuration has been finished, the tool has to be closed by choosing *Save and Exit* in the main menu. Following the command *make dep* has to be executed. This is necessary to generate the VHDL configuration file. If this is not done, the sources of the LEON 2 processor do not correspond to the configuration done before. The *make dep* command is only necessary after graphical configuration, when using *make config* this is done automatically.

5.2. Synthesis of LEON 2

After a configuration has been made, the synthesis can be started. The LEON 2 processor supports Synopsys DC, Xilinx ISE and Synplicity Synplify synthesis tools. For the Secure CPU project the tool Xilinx ISE 8.1i was used.

To start the synthesis *make fpga* has to be typed in the command line. This starts the synthesis for the board with the current configuration. To target other boards, the command line switch BOARD has to be added in a way like: *make fpga BOARD=gr-xc3s1500*. When using the non-graphical configuration mode, it is possible to combine the keywords *config* and *fpga* to make the synthesis more performing. For more synthesis switches browse the Makefile at top-level directory. If the synthesis had exited without errors, a bit stream file was generated at *leon2-1.0.32-xst/boards/$(BOARD)*. If any errors had occurred, they will be displayed on the command line. It is useful to redirect the outputs of the synthesis tools to a text file. This could be done by adding > *[filename]* at the end of the synthesis command. If the command *make config fpga BOARD=gr-cpci-xc2v > synthesis.log* is typed, all outputs of the synthesis tools are redirected to the file *synthesis.log* in the top-level directory.

5.3. Connection to LEON 2

After synthesis and loading the generated bit file to the Field Programmable Gate Array (FPGA), it is possible to connect to the LEON 2 processor. Gaisler Research provides a software called GRMON. It is available for Linux, Windows and Windows Cygwin. This software tool has two operating modes: command-line mode and GDB mode. In command-line mode, GRMON commands are entered manually through a terminal window. In GDB mode, GRMON acts as a GDB gateway and translates the GDB extended-remote protocol to debug commands on the target system. A rough block diagram of GRMON is shown in Figure 5-1. [35]

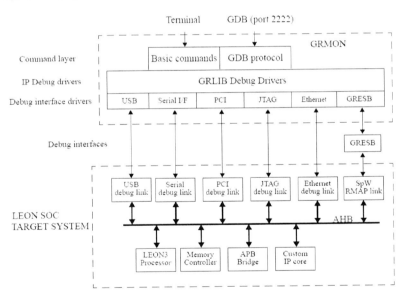

Figure 5-1: Block Diagram of GRMON [35]

There are many possibilities to connect with GRMON to the processor:

- Connect using the serial port or Ethernet
- Connect to the Joint Test Action Group (JTAG) Debug Link using Xilinx Parallel Cable III or IV or Universal Serial Bus (USB) debug link

Not all of these modes will work with LEON 2 processor, some of them are only available for other processors. The connection via the serial interface should work with all processors from Gaisler Research. So, this method was used to connect to the processor core in the project.

When starting GRMON in command-line mode without any parameters, it will try to connect to the Debug Support Unit (DSU) of the target system via the serial interface. To enable that, the DSU has to be activated in configuration. Some switches for DSU must be in correct setting and the serial interface module of the DSU (dcom0) must be connected to a serial port of the host. The LEON 2 processor supports three serial interfaces, two of them (*uart1* and *uart2*) are available for any user application and the interface (*dcom0*) is responsible for the communication with the DSU. The number of interfaces, which are available on a development board, depends on the available serial connectors. For connecting at least one, a serial null modem cable is needed, but some boards will need special cables to connect *uart1* and *dcom0*. This fact is discussed in section 5.4.4.

If a successful connection to LEON 2 can be established, a prompt will appear and GRMON waits for user input. The first steps after connecting via the serial interface are to check, if GRMON is able to communicate with the DSU. If GRMON reports *Warning: stack pointer not set* or *Cannot continue, processor not in debug mode*, this is an indication for a not correctly working DSU. In any case, there is a wrong configured DSU or any connection between the serial port of the host system and the serial port of the DSU not connected properly. Next, it is useful to execute the GRMON commands *info sys* and *info reg*, which will print detailed system respectively register information. If something is missing in this output, the configuration of the processor should be checked.

The start process of GRMON should look like as shown in Figure 5-2 in case of a correct working LEON 2 processor and DSU. After starting and verifying if the processor is working correct, a program or an operating system can be loaded into memory by the use of the command *load*.

```
GRMON LEON debug monitor v1.1.16 (evaluation version)

Copyright (C) 2004,2005 Gaisler Research - all rights reserved.
For latest updates, go to http://www.gaisler.com/
Comments or bug-reports to support@gaisler.com

try open device //./com1
###opened device //./com1

GRLIB plug&play not found, switching to LEON2 legacy mode

initialising ..........
detected frequency:  50 MHz
Device ID: : 65535
GRLIB build version: 65535

Component                          Vendor
LEON2 Memory Controller            European Space Agency
LEON2 SPARC V8 processor           European Space Agency
LEON2 Configuration register       European Space Agency
LEON2 Timer Unit                   European Space Agency
LEON2 UART                         European Space Agency
LEON2 UART                         European Space Agency
LEON2 Interrupt Ctrl               European Space Agency
LEON2 I/O port                     European Space Agency
AHB Debug UART                     Gaisler Research
LEON2 Debug Support Unit           Gaisler Research

grlib> info sys
00.04:00f   European Space Agency  LEON2 Memory Controller (ver 0)
            ahb: 00000000 - 20000000
            ahb: 20000000 - 40000000
            ahb: 40000000 - 80000000
            apb: 80000000 - 80000010
            8-bit prom @ 0x00000000
            32-bit sdram: 1 * 64 Mbyte @ 0x40000000, col 9, cas 2, ref 7.8 us
01.04:002   European Space Agency  LEON2 SPARC V8 processor (ver 0)
            apb: 80000014 - 80000018
02.04:008   European Space Agency  LEON2 Configuration register (ver 0)
            apb: 80000024 - 80000028
            val: e877bf00
03.04:006   European Space Agency  LEON2 Timer Unit (ver 0)
            apb: 80000040 - 80000070
04.04:007   European Space Agency  LEON2 UART (ver 0)
            apb: 80000070 - 80000080
            baud rate 38400
05.04:007   European Space Agency  LEON2 UART (ver 0)
            apb: 80000080 - 80000090
            baud rate 38400
06.04:005   European Space Agency  LEON2 Interrupt Ctrl (ver 0)
            apb: 80000090 - 800000a0
07.04:009   European Space Agency  LEON2 I/O port (ver 0)
            apb: 800000a0 - 800000ac
08.01:007   Gaisler Research  AHB Debug UART (ver 0)
            apb: 800000c0 - 800000d0
            baud rate 115200, ahb frequency 50.00
09.01:002   Gaisler Research  LEON2 Debug Support Unit (ver 0)
            ahb: 90000000 - a0000000
            trace buffer 512 lines, stack pointer 0x43fffff0
            CPU#0 win 8, hwbp 2, V8 mul/div, srmmu, lddel 1
                  icache 1 * 8 kbyte, 32 byte/line
                  dcache 1 * 8 kbyte, 32 byte/line
```

Figure 5-2: Start-Up and Check Sequence

After loading the Linux SnapGear operating system, which is shown in Figure
5-3, it could be started with the command run. This will set the PC and the NPC
and start the execution.

```
grlib> load image.dsu
        section: .stage2 at 0x40000000, size 6084 bytes
        section: .vmlinux at 0x40004000, size 1060928 bytes
        section: .rdimage at 0x4011c3f4, size 1865180 bytes
        section: .text at 0x402e39d0, size 220 bytes
        total size: 2932412 bytes (81.1 kbit/s)
        read 2171 symbols
        entry point: 0x40000000
```

Figure 5-3: Loading Operating System Image

If a terminal is connected to *uart1* of LEON 2 SnapGear will output the starting process. For other programs than SnapGear, it is possible to redirect this output to *dcom0*, which means that GRMON will handle the output data. This, so called loop-back mode, is useful if the board or the host system does not have two serial interfaces. It is activated by starting GRMON with the switch *−u*. Moreover, it is useful to start GRMON with the switch *−nb* when the MMU of LEON 2 is enabled, to avoid going into break mode on a page-fault or data exception.

```
signal rtsctsbridge : std_logic_vector(1 downto 0);
. . .
uart1i.rxd      <= pioo.rxd(0); uart1i.ctsn    <= rtsctsbridge(0);
uart2i.rxd      <= pioo.rxd(1); uart2i.ctsn    <= rtsctsbridge(1);
uart1i.scaler   <= pioo.io8lsb; uart2i.scaler  <= pioo.io8lsb;
. . .
rtsctsbridge(0) <= uart1o.rtsn;
rtsctsbridge(1) <= uart2o.rtsn;
```

Figure 5-4: RTS-CTS Bridge for Usage with SnapGear

When using the Linux distribution SnapGear, it is necessary to add two signal bridges in the LEON 2 source code between *rts* and *cts* of *uart1* and *uart2*. If this is not done, SnapGear is not able to finish the boot process and will stop while trying to change the baud rate of the serial interface. Therefore, the module *mcore.vhd* at *leon2-1.0.32-xst/leon* has to be changed and a signal *rtsctsbridge* has to added and connected properly. The changes are shown in Figure 5-4, where lines, which are marked as bold, were changed or were inserted.

5.4. XESS XSV800 (Virtex)

The XESS XSV800 development board is basically used for processing video and audio signals. Furthermore, it is a useable development platform for small soft processor core projects.

5.4.1. Board Features

The Xilinx XSV800 development board includes two programmable logic chips. The first chip is a Xilinx Virtex FPGA XCV800 containing roughly 888.000 system gates. It represents the main repository of programmable logic on the board. The second is used to manage the configuration of the Virtex FPGA via the parallel or serial port or the Flash RAM and is called Xilinx XC95108 Complex Programmable Logic Device (CPLD). It also controls the configuration of the Ethernet chip. This board also contains resources, which are shown in Figure 5-5 and listed below: [36]

- 2 MByte Flash RAM to store multiple configurations of the FPGA. Whenever the development board is powered up, the XCV800 can be programmed with the flash bit stream. After power-up this RAM can be used to store general-purpose data for the FPGA.

- 2 MByte SRAM divided into two independent banks on the scale of 512K x 16bits. They are used for general-purpose data storage.

- Programmable oscillator that provides a clock signal to the FPGA and the CPLD. The clock frequencies are derived from its maximum frequency of 100 MHz. The programmed divisor value is stored in the internal Electrically Erasable PROM (EEPROM), so it will be restored whenever the power is applied to the XSV board. Also an external clock could be added to the development board.

- Video decoder that digitizes National Television Systems Committee (NTSC), Phase Alternation Line (PAL) and other video signals and outputs the digitized data to the FPGA. To display a video signal on a monitor, a RAM Digital to Analog Converter (DAC) with a 24 bit colour map is used.

- Audio codec to digitize or generate stereo audio signals with up to 20 bits of resolution and a bandwidth of 50 KHz.

- Ethernet Physical Layer (PHY) chip to interface to an Ethernet Local Area Network (LAN) at up to 100 Mbps. This chip connects to both the FPGA and the CPLD. During an active connection to the network the FPGA manages the transfer of data packets to and from the PHY chip.

- Two 7-segment Light Emitting Diode (LED) digits and a 10-segment LED bar graph that displays status information about the FPGA and the CPLD.

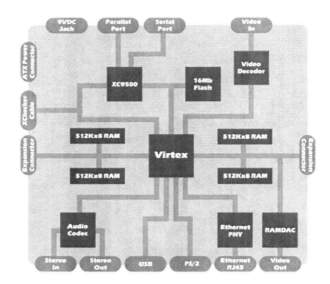

Figure 5-5: Block Diagram of Xilinx XSV800

The Xilinx XSV800 development board also provides different interfaces to communicate with the outside world: [36]

- PS/2 port to connect either a common keyboard or mouse device. The FPGA receives a clock signal and a serial data stream, synchronized with the falling edge of the clock signal.

- Single USB port to connect a variety of peripherals. It allocates a serial Input/Output (I/O) channel with bandwidths of 1.5 to 12 Mbps to the FPGA.

- One parallel and one serial port interface enable the CPLD to send and receive data in a parallel or serial format.

- Two independent 38 pin expansion ports connected to the FPGA.

The development board normally operates with +9V direct voltage provided from an external power supply. Voltage regulators will generate +2.5V for the Virtex FPGA core logic, +5V and +3.3V voltages for all other board components.

5.4.2. FPGA Features

The main programmable logic on the XESS XSV800 development board is a Virtex XCV800 FPGA. The device incorporates the following attributes in a 240-pin HQ240 package: [37]

- 888.439 system gates.

- 21.168 logic cells, representing the basic configurable logic unit within the FPGA. One of these cells consists of a 4-input Look-Up Table (LUT), a D-Flip-Flop and additional carry logic.

- 14 KBytes internal block-RAM, which can be used as global memory for the entire FPGA. Each block of the memory consists of 4096 bits, programmable from 4096 x 1 bit to 256 x 16 bit.

5.4.3. Synthesis for XSV800

Gaisler Research provides a template for configuration and synthesis of the XESS XSV800 board. Related files are available at *leon2-1.0.32-xst/boards/hecht-xsv800*. Before the configuration and synthesis can be done, some changes in source code have to be established.

- Change in *leon_xsv800.vhd* and *leon_eth_xsv800.vhd* from
  ```
  sddqm : out std_logic_vector (3 downto 0);
  ```
  to `sddqm : out std_logic_vector (7 downto 0);`

- Change in the Makefile located at *leon2-1.0.32-xst/syn/xst* from
  `DEVICE=xcv-hq240-6` to `DEVICE=xcv-hq240-4`

Leon_xsv800.vhd respectively *leon_eth_xsv800.vhd* are used to implement a top-level entity, which contains the component *leon* respectively *leon_eth*. This top-level entity is used to emphasize the ports, which are connected to the Xilinx XSV800 board. The pin assignments of the FPGA for the ports could be found at *leon.ucf* respectively *leon_eth.ucf*. The suffix *ucf* stands for User Constraints File.

5.4.4. Connection to XSV800

The XSV800 board from XESS has a parallel and a serial port. The parallel port is used to program the FPGA, for which the program GXSLOAD was used. The serial port is normally used to connect to the interface of the DSU (*dcom0*), as well as to the first serial interface (*uart1*).

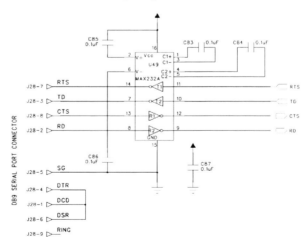

Figure 5-6: Serial Interface Schematic of XSV800 Board [38]

92

The schematic of the serial interface is shown in Figure 5-6. As illustrated, only TxD, RxD, RTS and CTS are usable for communication with the board. This signals are routed over a CPLD to the FPGA. A sample configuration for the CPLD could be found at *leon2-1.0.32-xst/boards/hecht-xsv800/cpld*. In this sample TxD and RxD are used for *uart1* and RTS and CTS are used for *dcom0*. The existing pin assignment of the LEON 2 processor core on the XSV800 board is shown in Figure 5-7.

LEON 2 Pin	CPLD Pin	RS232
uart1 rxd	80	RxD
uart1 txd	81	TxD
dcom0 dsurx	85	CTS
dcom0 dsutx	82	RTS

Figure 5-7: Pin Assignments of LEON 2 on XSV800 Board

To make this work, a special Y-cable, which splits TxD/RxD and RTS/CTS had to be build. This cable routes TxD and RxD of XSV800 RS232 to RxD and TxD of one RS232 connector as crossover, and RTS and CTS of XSV800 RS232 to RxD and TxD of another RS232 connector. The schematic of the Y-cable is shown in Figure 5-8.

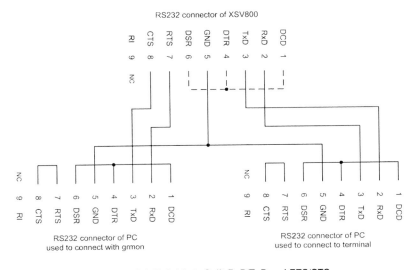

Figure 5-8: Y-Cable to Split RxD/TxD and RTS/CTS

The bridges between DCD, DTR and DSR respectively RTS and CTS on side of the computers are needed. The bridge between DCT, DTR and DSR on side of the XSV800 board (illustrated as dotted line in Figure 5-8) is not necessary, because these pins are never used.

If the first serial interface (*uart1*) is not needed or GRMON is started in loop-back mode, there is a second possibility how to connect to the XSV800 board. In that mode, it is possible to route txd/rxd of *uart1* to CTS/RTS of XSV800 RS232 and dsurx/dsutx of *dcom0* to RxD/TxD of XSV800 RS232. In this case a serial null crossover modem cable and a special CPLD configuration is needed. The CPLD is responsible for routing and so the pin assignments in *dwnldpar.ucf* at *leon2-1.0.32-xst/boards/hecht-xsv800/cpld* had to be changed. The new assignments are shown in Figure 5-9.

LEON 2 Pin	dwnldpar.ucf	CPLD Pin	RS232
uart1 rxd	RxD	80	CTS
uart1 txd	TxD	81	RTS
dcom0 dsurx	CTS	85	RxD
dcom0 dsutx	RTS	82	TxD

Figure 5-9: Pin assignments when using loop-back mode of GRMON

5.4.5. Programming of CPLD and FPGA on XSV800

To program the CPLD and the FPGA of the XESS XSV800 board the program GXSLOAD is used, which is part of the XSTOOLs provided by XESS. This software is available for Linux and Windows operating systems. GXSLOAD uses the parallel port to program chips on target boards. Only the CPLD is directly programmable via the parallel port. Programming of FPGA, Flash and RAM is done via the CPLD and a serial cable, because the parallel port has no direct connection to these components. Before programming the FPGA, it is necessary to program the CPLD. When programming the Flash or the RAM afterwards, this reprogramming of the CPLD is done automatically.

To program the CPLD, with the Windows version of GXSLOAD (shown in Figure 5-10), simply drag and drop the CPLD programming file *dwnldpar.svf* to the CPLD/FPGA section in GXSLOAD, then select Load.

After finishing the programming of the CPLD, the FPGA programming file, which was generated while synthesis, has to be selected and the loading process has to be started again. After finishing, the FPGA is loaded and GRMON should be able to connect to the processor via the serial interface.

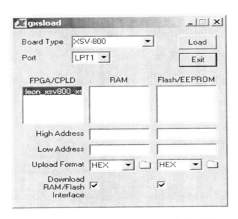

Figure 5-10: Graphical Interface of GXSLOAD

5.4.6. Generation of CPLD Programming File

To generate the CPLD programming file in Serial Vector Format (SVF), Xilinx ISE and Xilinx Impact is needed. After starting Xilinx ISE selecting the CPLD device of XSV800, named XC95108-TQ100-20, and the associated source code files, e.g. *dwnldpar.vhd* and *dwnldpar.ucf*, an ISE project with the desired CPLD device is created. After that step the synthesis can be started.

When this had succeeded, *Generate Programming File* has to be selected followed from *Generate SVF/XSVF/STAPL File*. The last action opens an assistant in Xilinx Impact. In this assistant *Prepare a Boundary-Scan* File and *CPLD Programming File* as file format have to be selected. Finally, the generated file has to be selected. After completing that step, the CPLD device can be programmed. It is recommended to erase the chip before. When this programming had succeeded a SVF file should be generated which could be used to program the CPLD device. The last step of the generation of a CPLD programming file is shown in Figure 5-11.

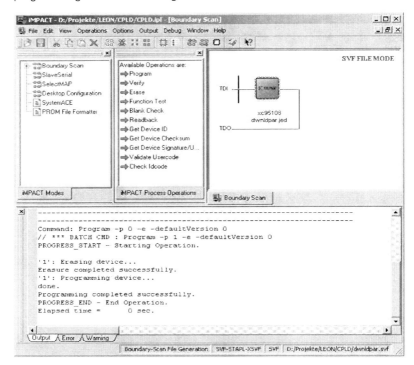

Figure 5-11: Generation of a CPLD programming file in Xilinx Impact

5.4.7.   Conclusion

The XSV800 development board was available at the University and so the usage does not result in any additional costs. Furthermore, the first implementation of a LEON 2 processor core was performed on that particular board. Considering the Secure CPU project, the Xilinx Virtex XCV800 FPGA is not suitable, because it provides an undersized internal Block-RAM and fewer system gates as necessary. Although an implementation of the original LEON 2 processor core was done on this board, the newly developed and secured LEON 2 processor core does not fit on the existing FPGA.

5.5. Pender GR-XC3S-1500 (Spartan 3)

The Pender GR-XC3S-1500 development board represents a platform, which enables the implementation of complex FPGA designs. It incorporates a high-capacity Xilinx Spartan-3 FPGA, a large on-board memory and a number of different communication interfaces on a compact Euro card format. It has been developed by Xilinx in cooperation with Gaisler Research to enable the evaluation of the LEON 2 and LEON 3 processor systems. This board includes all necessary features and interfaces for hardware and software development. [39]

5.5.1. Board Features

The GR-XC3S-1500 development board includes one programmable logic chip called Xilinx Spartan-3 XC3S-1500-4FG456 FPGA. It contains roughly 1.5 million system gates in size and represents the core of the development board. This board also contains resources, which are shown in Figure 5-12 and listed below: [39]

- One 500 KByte and one 125 KByte Xilinx Platform Flash Programmable ROM (PROM) to store an FPGA configuration in a non-volatile manner.

- 8 MByte Flash PROM to store executable programs for example an operating system. Upon power up, the processor will automatically arrange the execution of the program at location 0x00000000.

- 64 MByte Synchronous Static RAM (SDRAM) with 32 bits wide interface used by the FPGA for general-purpose data storage.

- 3 different oscillators including the 50 MHz main oscillator and a 25 MHz Ethernet clock. A DIL-8 socket is provided to allow the installation of a user defined oscillator to enable a second clock signal.

- High-Speed Video DAC device to drive a generated 50 MHz, 24 bit video signal to a standard 15 pin monitor connector interface.

- Dual-Speed Fast Ethernet PHY device to connect to an Ethernet LAN at up to 100 Mbps. To use this feature it is necessary to configure the Ethernet Media Access Control (MAC) function in the FPGA.

- 8 LED indicators. Four LEDs are user-programmable, the other indicate power, programming status, busy PROM and USB fault.

The board also provides different communication interfaces: [39]

- Two PS/2 ports to connect a common keyboard and mouse device.

- USB 2.0 transceiver to connect either a USB-A (Host) or a USB-B (Peripheral) type device. It operates either at 30 MHz or at 60 MHz depending on the jumper configuration on board.

- Two serial interfaces supporting data rates up to 1 MBaud. They can be configured to support program download and the LEON DSU for processor debugging.

- One 120-pin memory expansion connector to add for example a SRAM memory via a mezzanine board or to connect to logic analyser with a compatible adapter.

- JTAG interface to program the Xilinx platform Flash PROM and to configure the FPGA via a parallel cable III or a parallel cable IV.

The development board normally operates with + 5V direct voltage provided from an external power supply. An on-board power regulator will generate the following voltages: [39]

- + 3,3 V for the memory, interfaces and peripheral devices

- + 1,2 V for the FPGA core

- + 2,5 V auxiliary voltage required by the FPGA

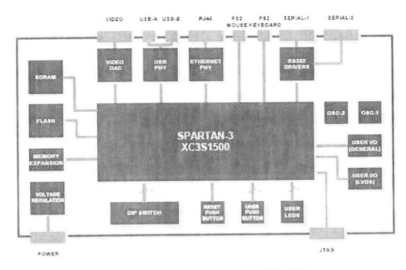

Figure 5-12: Block Diagram of GR-XC3S-1500

The Pender development board for LEON 2 and LEON 3 processor cores is shown in Figure 5-13.

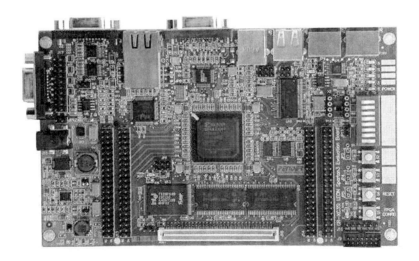

Figure 5-13: Pender Development Board

99

5.5.2. FPGA Features

A Xilinx Spartan-3 XC3S-1500-4FG456 FPGA represents the main repository of programmable logic on the GR-XC3S-1500 development board. It stands for a low-cost but high-performance logic device. The XC3S1500 device incorporates the following attributes: [40]

- 1.500.000 system gates

- 29.952 logic cells, representing the basic configurable logic unit.

- 72 KBytes internal block-RAM, which can be used as global memory for the entire FPGA. This memory is divided into independent blocks, which have a maximum capacity of 18 Kbits, respectively 16 Kbits without the usage of parity lines. Each block has a dual port structure, whereas each port has its own data, control and clock lines for synchronous read and write operations.

- 32 embedded multipliers that accept two input words, either in an 18 bit signed or a 17 bit unsigned form and produce a 36 bit output, to support read/multiply/accumulate operations.

- 4 Digital Clock Managers (DCM) to easily generate user specific clocks with varying frequencies and phases within the FPGA. Therefore, each DCM supports a clock skew elimination, a frequency synthesis and a phase shifting.

5.5.3. Synthesis for GR-XC3S-1500

Gaisler Research also provides templates for configuration and synthesis for the GR-XC3S-1500 board. This files could be found at *leon2-1.0.32-xst/boards/gr-xc3s1500*. So, the synthesis can be done with default settings. Based on this file, two more configurations files were generated. The file *config-nommu* represents a configuration of LEON 2 without using a MMU. The other file *config-mmu* represents a configuration with using a MMU. The used configuration settings are illustrated in Figure 5-14.

		config-nommu	config-mmu
Interger Unit	Register windows	8	
	MUL/DIV instructions avaiable	Yes	
	Hardware multiplier latency	5 cycles	
	Load delay	1	
	Hardware watchpoints	2	
Cache System	Number of sets	1	1
	Set size (kbytes/set)	8	8
	Line size (bytes/line)	32	32
	Enable local instruction RAMs	No	-
Memory Management Unit	Enable MMU	No	Yes
	MMU type	-	Combined
	TLB replacement sheme	-	Increment
	TLB entries	-	8
	Enable Diagnostic access	-	No
Debug Support Unit	Enable DSU	Yes	
	Trace buffer	Yes	
	Mixed instruction/AHB tracing	Yes	
	Trace buffer lines	512	
Memory Controller	8 bit PROM/SRAM bus support	Yes	
	16 bit PROM/SRAM bus support	No	
	RAM write protection	No	
	Write strobe timing feedback	No	
	5th SRAM chip-select	No	
	SDRAM controller	Yes	
	Inverted SDRAM clock	No	
	Separate address and data buses	No	
	64 bit SDRAM bus	No	
Peripherals	LEON configuration register	Yes	
	Secondary interrupt controller	No	
	Watchdog	No	
	AHB status register	No	
	On-chip AHB RAM	No	
	Ethernet interface	No	
	PCI interface	No	
Boot options	Boot selection	Memory	

Figure 5-14: LEON 2 Configuration Settings for GR-XC3S-1500

5.5.4. Connection to GR-XC3S-1500

The GR-XC3S-1500 board has two serial and one JTAG interfaces. The serial interfaces are used to connect the DSU (*dcom0*) on the one hand and the first serial interface of LEON 2 (*uart1*) on the other hand. As a result, it is not necessary to merge the signals of *dcom0* and *uart1* to a single serial interface, because there are enough serial interfaces available. Serial cables have to be used, where RxD and TxD are not crossed and these cables are in scope of delivery of GR-XC3S-1500 board.

101

The JTAG interface is used to program the FPGA and the two flashes, which can be used to store a non-volatile configuration of the FPGA. The programming is also accomplished with Xilinx Impact. The connection between the board and Impact could be established in three ways:

- Using a Xilinx Parallel Cable IV ribbon cable.

- Using a Parallel Cable IV flying leads cable.

- Using a low-cost JTAG programming cable (Parallel Cable III).

The last cable is in the scope of delivery of GR-XC3S-1500 board, so it was used for programming and monitoring the board.

5.5.5. Programming of FPGA on GR-XC3S-1500

There are two possibilities how to load a configuration into the FPGA. The first is to load it automatically at power up from the provided flashes (Master Serial Mode Configuration). The second is to load it normally via the JTAG interface (JTAG Mode Configuration). Which mode is active is depending on the jumper settings of JP9 on the development board. JTAG Mode Configuration is active when jumpers J9 1-2 and 5-6 are set. Otherwise Master Serial Mode Configuration is active.

After starting Xilinx Impact and detecting the hardware chain, the software should show three devices: two platform flashes (*xcf04s* and *xcf01s_vo20*) and one FPGA (*xc3s1500*). Next the configuration files have to be assigned and the devices have to be programmed.

For programming it is useful to select the option *Verify*. In that case the programmed device is verified, if it has been correctly written. Therefore, the files *leon*.ll* and *leon*.msk*, which were created while synthesis, are needed. The associated screenshot of Xilinx Impact is shown in Figure 5-15. Programming files for the flashes are also created by using Xilinx Impact. Therefore, *Prepare a PROM File* has to be selected after starting of Xilinx Impact. Next *Xilinx PROM* has to be set as target and *MCS* as file.

In the next step the existing flash devices have to be selected in the correct order. In case of GR-XC3S-1500 this means that the device *xcf04s* has position one and the device *xcf01s_vo20* has position two.

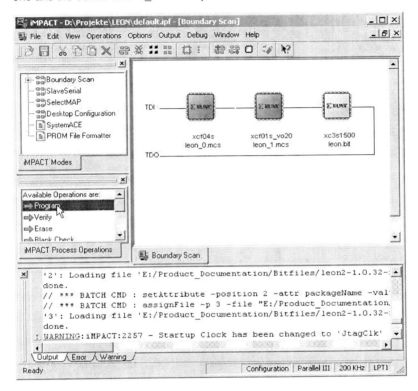

Figure 5-15: Programming Flash of GR-XC3S-1500

Next, the source for the PROM configuration has to be selected. In case of storing a FPGA configuration in PROM this will be bit stream file. Note that Xilinx Impact will ask to add another device to the chain after assigning the bit stream file, but in case of Secure CPU this is not necessary. The last step in programming the PROM files is to select *Generate File*, which will create the needed files. The associated screenshot of Xilinx Impact, including the programming chain, is shown in Figure 5-16.

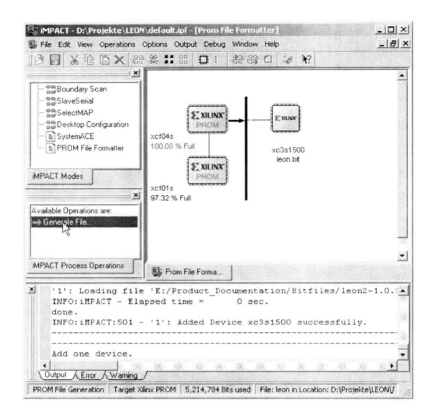

Figure 5-16: Chain for programming the PROM files

5.5.6. Programming of FLASH on GR-XC3S-1500

The GR-XC3S-1500 development board contains another platform flash, which can be used as non-volatile memory. Programming of this 8 MByte flash is also done via the software tool GRMON. For detection, if there is any flash, GRMON command *flash* can be used. This command will print any available information of the flash. An excerpt of the provided information is shown in Figure 5-17.

```
Intel-style 8-bit flash on D[31:24]

Manuf.    Intel
Device    MT28F640J3
Device ID 3878ffff03005141
User   ID ffffffffffffffff

1 x 8 Mbyte = 8 Mbyte total @ 0x00000000

CFI info
flash family  : 1
flash size    : 64 Mbit
erase regions : 1
erase blocks  : 64
write buffer  : 32 bytes
region  0     : 64 blocks of 128 KBytes
```

Figure 5-17: GRMON Flash Information

Before programming the flash, it is necessary to erase it. This is done by using a given command in GRMON. After successful erasing, programming can be started by loading the flash. A useful selection of commands is shown in Figure 5-18.

```
flash                      // Detect flash
flash unlock all           // Unlock flash
flash erase all            // Erase flash
flash load <filename>      // Load file into flash
flash verify               // Verify loaded flash file
flash lock all             // Lock flash
```

Figure 5-18: GRMON Flash Commands

5.5.7.   Conclusion

This board is specifically designed for educational use and represents a low-cost development platform. Additional the delivered package includes JTAG programming cables and synthesis software tools. This board was not available at the University, so it was necessary to order it from a reseller, called Pender Electronics, in Switzerland. The final price, minus an educational discount, including taxes and shipping costs from the named reseller were less than € 1,000 and therefore affordable for the project.

Regarding to the Secure CPU project, the GR-XC3S-1500 development board, including its Xilinx Spartan-3 FPGA, represents the best development environment. The device provides enough internal Block-RAM and system gates to upload the modified and secured version of the LEON 2 processor core on this FPGA. As a result, it was used for the final implementation.

5.6. Selection of Software Environment

The evaluation and selection of the operating system and CIL Compiler was done in a separate project work and will not be discussed in this book. As an overview, the Linux distribution SnapGear, which is specially compiled for LEON processors, was used in conjunction with portable.NET. The system architecture is shown in Figure 5-19.

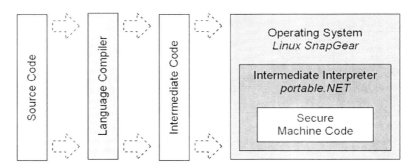

Figure 5-19: System Architecture

The CIL interpreter of portable.NET was modified to the needs of the new processors and restrictions of the modified instruction set architecture. Therefore, additional commands were added and integrated arithmetic checking code was removed. The Common Language Infrastructure (CLI), which is part of the Microsoft .NET strategy, enables an application program written in any of several commonly-used programming languages to be run on any operating system using a common runtime environment rather than a language-specific one. CLI provides a virtual execution environment comparable to the one provided by Sun Microsystems for Java programs. In both environments, CLI and Java, a compiler is used to process the source code into a preliminary form of executable code, called byte code. When a program is executed, its byte code is compiled on the fly into native code, which is required by the machine architecture of a given computer. CLI has been accepted as an open standard by ECMA, an international organization for the promotion of technology standards.

6. Implementation

This chapter includes the current implementation of secure bound checking, secure bound storage and secure exception handling. Moreover, not implemented approaches, which were necessary for the development of the final solution, are discussed.

6.1. Secure Bound Checking

When implementing the defined design, which was discussed in section 3.1, it had to be decided, where the comparator unit should reside. In a complex structure, as the SPARC V8, the location of this unit is very important, because it needs certain information provided by the Integer Unit (IU) on one hand, as well as data and addresses from the memory on the other hand. The integration of a completely new part into an already implemented processor core causes certain issues. A pipelined processor has to follow a defined timing concept, resulting from the number of stages integrated. Several approaches were worked out and so, the comparator unit was integrated in external and internal locations. Each implementation had to be proven, whether it is applicable and provides good performance and security.

6.1.1. External Comparator

The first approach was an external comparator unit. The problem of buffer overflows arises, if the IU loads data from a location outside a defined range. Access should also not be granted, if the IU writes data to a position in the memory that has not been initialized before. When reading, as well as writing accesses are secured, the whole system should be secured.

Basically, the IU obtains all data from the data cache (memory) and delivers data to it, as well. As a result, a good location for a comparator unit would be between IU and data cache. Its function would force every data transaction from IU to data cache, to be valid. The validity of such a transaction would be assured by each value passing through and being compared with the associated bounds. This comparison should be realized by two hardware comparators, checking the value to be located in-between a certain range, which is described by its two bounds. A draft block diagram of the proposed data path comparator, which is located outside the IU, is shown in Figure 6-1.

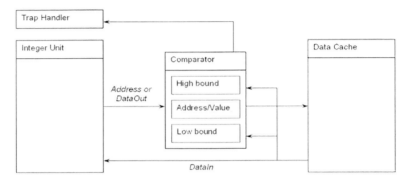

Figure 6-1: External Data Path Comparator

Regarding the external data path comparator, the operation of bound checking consists of two phases: Firstly, the data values (current value, low bound and high bound) have to be fetched and transferred into the proper registers. This includes the calculation of addresses representing the position in main memory of the value and its associated bounds. Since the data cache provides only one output port, these three data values have to be loaded serially. Secondly, the current value is compared to the low, as well as the high bound simultaneously and if not equal a trap is triggered.

The main issue of this architecture was the loading operation. If the data is loaded from the comparator unit, this architecture had to contain an intelligent sequence control. It would have to include a small ALU that adapts the address of the current value. These adapted addresses would have to be sent to the data cache serially. The data would drop in continuously and force the IU to wait until the data has arrived and has been validated as being correct. Furthermore, there must be a possibility to store the bounds information in registers. Otherwise the bounds have to be loaded for each load and store operation and the existing ones would simply be overwritten.

Though, the architecture could manage timing issues by a slight adaptation. So, all data could be loaded by the IU. This new loading mechanism would also represent a solution for the storage problem. If the data is loaded via the ALU, it has to pass the processor pipeline, which minimizes the additional efforts for register storage. Moreover, this adaptation includes the advantage of the address calculation in the existing ALU. Additional intelligence of the comparator unit itself is no longer necessary, but it includes the disadvantage that every piece of data has to pass through the comparator unit. The comparator unit needs information about all data, which is passing through it. Furthermore, a decision has to be made, whether the data has to be checked or not. The information could be delivered from the IU, but additional connections from IU to the data cache, as well as adaptations of the IU would be needed. Another disadvantage is that each processed data value needs two additional cycles (one for address and the other for the value). Concluding, the proposed data path comparator would result in a bad performance and many modifications in the processor core. Concluding, the current approach would be absolutely a possible solution, but it was not continued for developing the Secure CPU. However, some of the positive aspects of the first proposal were taken to the second.

6.1.2. Internal Comparator

The second concept was invented by improving the positive aspects of the first approach. Firstly, the position of the comparator unit was moved from outside to an additional stage in the IU pipeline. This decision was taken to minimize the effort of information transfer from and to the IU. In contrast to the external unit, an implementation in the IU itself guarantees that all information about data validity can be directly accessed.

The LEON 2 implements a five staged standard Reduced Instruction Set Computing (RISC) pipeline. To keep the VHDL code clean, as well as to keep the design concise, an additional stage was introduced. This stage, which consists of additional registers and hardware comparators, prevents the data cache from loading information from invalid storage locations, as well as the IU to send data to invalid addresses. Address calculations happen in the execution stage by the use of the ALU. At this position in the pipeline, also array accesses are implemented. The memory address is calculated by summing up the base address and a particular offset. Since this offset can be any number, the calculated address may be out-of-range. Next, the combined address is handed over to the memory stage. This stage is responsible to transfer data to the data cache. From the moment the data cache got the data, security prevention can not be established anymore. Therefore, the comparison must be carried out between address calculation and delivery. As a result, the check stage should be located between execution and memory stage. After the address calculation the result is delivered to the check stage, where the bound check will be done. In case of validity, the processed data is delivered to the memory stage. Otherwise the check stage will send a signal that triggers a trap. A block diagram of the modified pipeline, including the check stage, is shown in Figure 6-2.

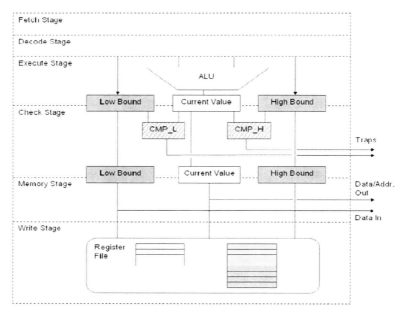

Figure 6-2: LEON 2 with Check Stage

The location for the additional check stage should guarantee the consistency of data being read from memory, as well as it secures the writing process by checking every address. Invalid addresses can not be overwritten nor being read. By securing the read and write process, the write stage and the register contents are secured as well. The issue of misusing data in form of invalid addresses is prevented by the check after the address calculation.

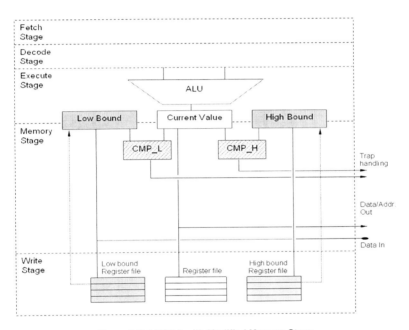

Figure 6-3: LEON 2 with Modified Memory Stage

Concerning timing problems arising from the implementation of a new stage in the LEON 2 pipeline, the functionality of the check stage was directly included in the memory stage. The functionality keeps the same, as explained previously and the new secure processor architecture is still SPARC V8 compliant. The new block diagram, including the modifications of the memory stage is shown in Figure 6-3.

6.1.3. Hardware Comparator

A hardware comparator is a simple architecture, where the input data is stored in registers, which will be compared bit-wise afterwards. If one input is smaller than the other, the output produces a signal of 1. Otherwise a signal 0 means that the comparison could be completed without any bound violations. The VHDL source code of a single comparator unit is shown in Figure 6-4.

```
library ieee;
use IEEE.std_logic_1164.all;
use IEEE.std_logic_arith.all;

entity comp is
        port (
                compi1 : in std_logic_vector(31 downto 0);
                compi2 : in std_logic_vector(31 downto 0);
                compo : out std_logic
        );
end comp;

architecture rtl of comp is
begin
        comp0: process(compi1, compi2)
                begin
                        if (compi1 < compi2) then
                                compo <= '1';
                        else
                                compo <= '0';
                        end if;
        end process;
end rtl;
```

Figure 6-4: VHDL Code of Compare Unit

The compare unit must be able to check if the address of an array element is in the range, defined by the array bounds. So, it consists of two hardware comparators, which are connected to the inputs and trap handler ports. The rough block diagram of the compare unit is shown in Figure 6-5.

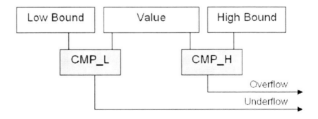

Figure 6-5: Block Diagram of Compare Unit

One comparator checks against the low bound and the other one against the high bound. This can be done simultaneously, because there are two individual hardware units. Although the outputs could be merged with a logical gate, it was decided to use both results and let them trigger different traps. This would allow different handling of the under- and overflow violations. The component generation of a compare unit, as well as the used port mappings are shown in Figure 6-6.

```
-- Component Generation
component comp
port (
        compi1 : in std_logic_vector(31 downto 0);
        compi2 : in std_logic_vector(31 downto 0);
        compo : out std_logic
);
end component;

-- Port Mapping
comp0 : comp port map(comp_value, comp_low, comp_out_low);
comp1 : comp port map(comp_high, comp_value, comp_out_high);
```

Figure 6-6: VHDL Code of Compare Unit

6.1.4.   Comparator Unit Enabling

Since a commercially available operating system for the LEON 2 processor was used, it did not include bound information. This means that the compare unit has to be switched off while executing operating system and legacy code. A check with non-existing bounds would never validate and this would force the operating system to crash on each boot. Therefore, the comparator unit must implement a mechanism, which allows the unit to be switched off. Furthermore, it should be possible to use the bound checking feature only on demand. Each piece of code should seamlessly be checked if bounds are used or not. If bounds do not exist, there is also no reason for checking. Currently, no methods exist, which inform the system of the non-existence of bounds. As a consequence, the checking unit is turned off by default and to turn it on, a trigger is necessary. This triggering happens after successfully loading the bounds from memory, because each bound is stored with a special bit, called valid-bit, giving information about its existence and validity. As a result, the trigger to enable the comparator unit will be fired automatically, as far as a valid-bit is present and set properly.

```
if(op = LDST and (op3 = LLB or op3 = LHB)) then
      bound_data := '1' & wrdata;
else
      bound_data := (others => '0');
end if;
```

Figure 6-7: VHDL Code to Set the Valid-Bit

The VHDL code, which sets the valid-bit to the address in the write stage, is shown in Figure 6-7. Only if the data, which is loaded into the comparator as high or low bound, verifies the valid-bit by proving its validity. So, the traps for under- and overflow are only triggered, when valid bounds exist and the valid-bit can be analyzed successfully. Otherwise the results are discarded. The block diagram, to enable trap triggering of the compare unit, is shown in Figure 6-8.

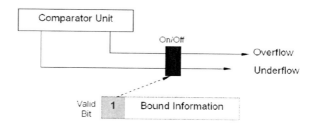

Figure 6-8: Compare Unit Enabling

6.1.5.   Internal Bound Storage in Register Files

Register files represent an easy way to handle numerous registers. In the SPARC V8 architecture, they are implemented as fast static RAMs. These files provide two read and one write ports. The ports can be unlocked by enable bits. Resulting of the two read ports, reading from two values can be established simultaneously. Though, only one value can be written at a particular time. This mal-conception hindered an effort of using only one additional register file for both, low and high bounds. The problem of addressing could have easily been circumvented by adding one bit to the address. This bit would have been 1 for high bounds and 0 for low bounds.

114

For that and the inability of simultaneous writing of two values the implementation was done using two additional register files. Therefore, the original register files architecture had to be adapted. The bound information has to include an additional bit that carries the information about the validity. So, a broader data bus to the register file had to be implemented. The needed VHDL code of a bound register file component, as well as the adapted types *rfb_in_type* and *rfb_out_type* are shown in Figure 6-9. The adapted types were used to realise the needed interfaces to the bound register file.

```
type rfb_in_type is record
        rdladdr  : std_logic_vector(RABITS-1 downto 0);    -- Read Address 1
        rd2addr  : std_logic_vector(RABITS-1 downto 0);    -- Read Address 2
        wraddr   : std_logic_vector(RABITS-1 downto 0);    -- Write Address
        wrdata   : std_logic_vector(RBDBITS-1 downto 0);   -- Write Data
        ren1     : std_logic;                              -- Read 1 Enable
        ren2     : std_logic;                              -- Read 2 Enable
        wren     : std_logic;                              -- Write Enable
end record;

type rfb_out_type is record
        data1            : std_logic_vector(RBDBITS-1 downto 0); -- read data 1
        data2            : std_logic_vector(RBDBITS-1 downto 0); -- read data 2
end record;

component bounds_regfile_iu
generic (
        rftype : integer := 1;
        abits : integer := 8; dbits : integer := 33; words : integer := 128
);

port (
        rst  : in std_logic;
        clk  : in clk_type;
        clkn : in clk_type;
        rfbi : in rfb_in_type;
        rfbo : out rfb_out_type);
end component;
```

Figure 6-9: VHDL Code of Bound Register File

Figure 6-10 illustrates the port mapping of the register file *rf0* and both bound register files *rfbl0* and *rfbh0*, as well as the definition of the new constant *RBDBITS*. The illustration of the register files is shown in Figure 6-3, which is discussed in section 6.1.2.

```
constant RBDBITS : integer := RDBITS + 1;

rf0 :     regfile_iu generic map (RFIMPTYPE, RABITS, RDBITS, IREGNUM)
          port map (rst, clk, clkn, rfi, rfo);
rfbl0 :   bounds_regfile_iu generic map (RFIMPTYPE, RABITS, RBDBITS, IREGNUM)
          port map (rst, clk, clkn, rfbli, rfblo);
rfbh0 :   bounds_regfile_iu generic map (RFIMPTYPE, RABITS, RBDBITS, IREGNUM)
          port map (rst, clk, clkn, rfbhi, rfbho);
```

Figure 6-10: VHDL Code of Register File Port Mapping

6.1.6. Instruction Set Modification

The original *LD* instruction was adapted to do loading, as well as resetting of bounds for debugging. In-fact the instruction does not write one register, it writes three registers having the same destination address. Since the bounds have to be loaded each time an element is read, they have to be reset after the operation. That means, the bound information is outdated and has to be set invalid.

This is done in the write stage, when writing the information from memory to the destination. The same register address can be used to find the correct location in the proper register file, because the bounds of an element are stored at the same destination in different register files. The only difference of the write operations is that the whole bound element is set to 0. This means that the bound information, as well as its valid-bit are 0. The used VHDL code is shown in section 6.1.4 in Figure 6-7.

Furthermore, there is a need for additional *LD* instructions. The purpose is to get the bounds from the memory into their proper bound registers. The instructions of LEON 2 are implemented in the whole pipeline. So, there is not a single place, where to find the implementation of an instruction. During execution of such an instruction, the instructions op-code is checked several times and accordingly certain flags are set and unset. Re-implementing of instructions should not be underestimated, because the complete pipeline progress has to be reconstructed. In this case, the *LD* instruction had to be pursued throughout the pipeline. Since the LD instruction is a member of the important *LDST* instruction group, it was also necessary to check all positions where a *LDST* flag is set.

The major difference between the default *LD* instruction and the newly introduced *Load Low Bound (LLB)* and *Load High Bound (LHB)* instructions is their destination register file. Whenever a bound loading instruction is executed, the data is written into a register in a bound register file. Furthermore, another instruction, called *Clear Bounds (CB)* was introduced to initialise the memory lines in a particular bound register file.

116

```
-- Additional LDH and LDL Commands for Loading Associated Bounds
constant LLB : std_logic_vector(5 downto 0) := "001000";
constant LHB : std_logic_vector(5 downto 0) := "011000";

-- Additional CB Command to Initialise Bound Register Files
constant CB  : std_logic_vector(5 downto 0) := "111000";
```

Figure 6-11: Additional Instructions

The definition of the additionally implemented instructions, which was done in the *sparcv8.vhd* source file, is shown in Figure 6-11. Moreover, new instruction codes had to be implemented into several positions of the execute stage. The VDHL source code modifications of the execute stage are shown in Figure 6-12.

```
-- Decoding of Load and Store Instructions
when LDST =>
        ...
        case op3 is
                -- added instructions LHB, LLB and CB
                when LD | LLB | LHB | CB | LDA | LDF | LDC => ld_size := LDWORD;
                ...
        ...

-- Do not write Data Cache for LLB, LHB and CB
when LDST =>
        ...
        if ((ctrl.trap or (wrin.ctrl.trap and not wrin.ctrl.annul)) = '0') and
           not (op3 = LLB or op3 = LHB or op3 = CB) then
                ...
        ...
```

Figure 6-12: VHDL Modifications in Execute Stage

The compare unit needs the bounds for its ability to check ranges. As described in section 3.1, bound registers should be statically connected to the compare unit. Once again the register file implementation shows its practical usage. Instead of connecting every bound register to the compare unit, resulting in the necessity of additional multiplexers, it is possible to achieve the same functionality by connecting only one interface. The connection is between the data port *r2* of the bound register files and one source port of each comparator unit.

As soon as an *LD* instruction is decoded the corresponding bounds should be loaded into the compare unit. This functionality can easily be provided by using the adapted *LD* destination address as the bound load address. So, the bound values are transferred to the compare unit and can be checked, as well as in case of bound violations, traps can be triggered immediately.

6.2. Secure Bound Storage

This section contains implementation approaches of storing bounds in memory securely. Moreover, the usage of a SPARC V8 reference MMU is considered to store bound information and secure meta data in memory.

6.2.1. Memory Management Unit

The LEON 2 processor core contains a MMU, which enables addressing of larger address spaces. The unit is based on the SPARC V8 reference MMU architecture. When the MMU is activated, a virtual address, which is provided by the processor, is translated to a physical address and passed to the memory controller, otherwise the virtual address is equal to the physical address and is passed directly to the memory controller. The architecture implements among other the following features: [30]

- 32 bit virtual and 36 bit physical address

- Fixed 4 KByte page size

- Support for large linear mappings and multiple contexts

- Page-level protections and hardware miss processing

The SPARC V8 MMU implements a three-level mapping. This means that three hierarchies of linked pages tables exist: Level-1, Level-2 and Level-3 page tables. An entry in a Level-1 table could point to the beginning of a Level-2 table and the entries in this table could again point to the beginning of the Level-3 tables. The root pointer, which points to the beginning of the Level-1 table, is located in the Context Table.

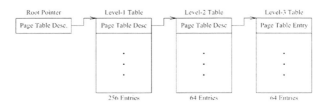

Figure 6-13: Three-level mapping used by MMU of SPARC V8 [30]

118

As shown in Figure 6-13, Level-1 tables contain 256 entries and Level-2 respectively Level-3 tables contain 64 entries each. The address space of one context is 4 GByte (256*64*64*4 KByte). Each entry in a page table has a length of 4 Byte, so the tables will need approximately 4 MByte. The last significant two bits of such an entry are used to distinguish the different types of a Page Table Entry (PTE), as shown in Figure 6-14. For SPARC V8 three-level mapping, a PTE could either be a link to the beginning of another page table or a link to a physical page itself. In the first case, the entry would be a Page Table Descriptor (PTD) and in the second case, it would be a PTE. This distinction is necessary because PTD and PTE are having different structures. The higher 30 bits of a PTD are used to store the Page Table Pointer (PTP). This pointer contains the physical address of the next-level page table. This address is in addition with a part of the virtual address used to calculate the address of the next selected entry out of the next page table.

Entry Type	Content
0 (00)	Invalid
1 (01)	Page Table Descriptor (PTD)
2 (10)	Page Table Entry (PTE)
3 (00)	Reserved

Figure 6-14: Entry Types of Page Table Entries [30]

The structure of a page table entry is shown in Figure 6-15.

Figure 6-15: Structure of Page Table Entries [30]

The virtual address is composed of three indices and one page offset, which is illustrated in Figure 6-16. The indices are used as offset in the three page tables to select a particular PTD or PTE.

Index 1	Index 2	Index 3	Page Offset
31 24	23 18	17 12	11 0

Figure 6-16: Structure of Virtual Addresses [30]

The page offset is used to select a specific entry out of a page in the physical address. Therefore, the Page Offset is appended to the end of the Physical Page Number (PPN). These two entries are building the physical address which is provided to the memory controller. So, it is possible to address 16,777,216 pages, having a size of 4 KByte each. This results in a physical address space of 64 GByte.

The PPN is part of each PTE. In a PTE the higher 24 bits are used to store the PPN and is needed to calculate the physical addresses. The remaining 6 bits are used to store different status types for each page. An overview of the status types is shown in Figure 6-17.

Shortcut	Name	Description
C	Cacheable	Set to one, if page is cacheable
M	Modified	Set to one, if page is accessed for writing
R	Referenced	Set to one, if page is accessed
ACC	Access	Indication access permissions

Figure 6-17: Status Types in Page Table Entries

The Access (ACC) field, which is shown in Figure 6-18, defines different access permissions for a page and so it is possible to restrict the accesses to it. It depends on the current processor mode (user or supervisor mode) and the access rights for this page, which process is able to access a page.

ACC	Accesses Allowed	
	User access	Supervisor access
0	Read Only	Read Only
1	Read/Write	Read/Write
2	Read/Execute	Read/Execute
3	Read/Write/Execute	Read/Write/Execute
4	Execute Only	Execute Only
5	Read Only	Read/Write
6	No Access	Read/Execute
7	No Access	Read/Write/Execute

Figure 6-18: Access Permissions for SPARC V8 Pages [30]

Each context has a unique context number and a unique address space. Additionally, there has to be a table were all root pointers, which are also called Root Pointer PTDs, to the Level-1 tables are stored.

This table is called Context Table. To identify the current active address space for a context, the context number is used as offset in the context table. The maximal number of available contexts is implementation-dependent, so the size of the context tables is also implementation-dependent. In case of the LEON 2 processor, the maximal number of contexts is eight and the context table will need 32 Byte. Concluding, the memory accesses would be too slow if the MMU every time needs to go through the three levels of page tables to translate a virtual address.

The main components of the SPARC V8 Reference MMU are the Virtual Address Latch, the Page Descriptor Cache and the MMU Register File. The first provides the Virtual Page Number and the Page Offset, the second stores the last used PTE and the last contains registers for storing the MMU status.

The operation of the MMU is simplified the following: Firstly, the virtual address is provided to the MMU and is stored in the Virtual Address Latch. Next the MMU looks at the Page Descriptor Cache, if there is any cached entry. So, the Virtual Page Number is compared with the Context Tags which correspond to the selected Virtual Address Tags. If there is a hit, the PPN found at the Page Descriptor Cache as well as the Page Offset stored at the Virtual Address Latch are tied up to the address bus. If there is no match, the MMU fetches the PTDs until it reaches the needed PTE. Otherwise is has to provide an proper error message.

6.2.2. Implementation of the SecureTag

Basically there are many possibilities for the realisation of a SecureTag implementation in a LEON 2 processor environment. Firstly, the SecureTag can be implemented in an additional data structure in existing memory chips. Secondly, an implementation in an additional memory chip is possible, which means a separated physical memory space. Finally, the SecureTag can be stored in the page tables or page table entries, in case of using a MMU.

To store the SecureTag in existing memory chips was rejected, because designing new chips is too expensive and would not be accepted by the industry. A way of implementing the SecureTag in additional memory chips is to use the local AHB RAM or to use an adapted memory controller. In both cases the size of this data structure is restricted by the LEON 2 configuration. If a MMU is used an implementation of the SecureTag in the page tables or page table entries is particularly possible. In that case, the SecureTag could be included in a data structure, which is needed anyway. To make this work a change in the page table layout of the LEON 2 MMU would be necessary. Another problem is that the program or operating system, which fills the memory with any content, needs to be changed.

It is only possible to set the SecureTag properly during the loading phase. This means that for a proper implementation, a change of GRMON and in case of using an operating system, also changes at the software level are needed. Additionally, when implementing the SecureTag in the page tables the changes in the LEON 2 MMU have to be considered in the operating system too. The necessary changes are very complex and time-consuming at the moment. The used software environment provides meta data directly to the register files in the processor core. As a result, a bound storage in the register files (discussed in section 6.1.2) was realised and the SecureTag technique in memory chips or page tables has not been considered yet.

6.3. Secure Exception Handling

The LEON 2 processor implements the default trap model of the SPARC architecture. This means that all traps have to be precise except for the following terms: [30]

- Exceptions caused by the FPU or the CP may be deferred traps.

- Exceptions, which make it impossible to return into the condition when the trap was caused, can be interrupting or deferred traps.

- Exceptions caused by an event, unrelated to the sequence of instructions are interrupting traps.

6.3.1. Trap Controlling

All possible traps are controlled by two fields, which are located in the PSR, shown in Figure 6-19: [30]

- Enable Traps (ET)

- Processor Interrupt Level (PIL)

impl	ver	icc	reserved	EC	EF	PIL	S	PS	ET	CWP
31:28	27:24	23:20	19:14	13	12	11:8	7	6	5	4:0

Figure 6-19: Structure of Processor Status Register

The ET bit has to be set to enable the handling of exceptions and interrupts. While ET is equal to 1, the IU prioritizes the outstanding exceptions and interrupts during the execution of instructions. This is done accordingly to the LEON 2 trap table. So, only the highest priority exception or interrupt request is considered as trap. Furthermore, the SPARC V8 architecture assumes that lower priority interrupts will persist and lower priority exceptions will recur, if the instruction, causing the exception, is executed again. [30]

The PIL field specifies the boundary, whether interrupt requests are accepted or not. The IU compares it with the level of a requested interrupt. If the PIL is lower, the processor triggers the trap, assuming that there are no higher priority exceptions at the moment. If the requested interrupt level is equal to fifteen, the processors always triggers the trap, presumed ET is equal to 1. While ET equals 0, all interrupt requests are ignored. If a trap occurs the processor stops execution and enters an error mode state without saving any state information in the local registers. After entering this state, the processor typically triggers an external reset to set the PC to the start address of the operating system.

6.3.2. LEON 2 Trap Table

The trap table, shown in Figure 6-20, contains an excerpt of trap types and the corresponding priorities, implemented in the LEON 2 processor.

Priority (Pri.) 1 is representing the highest priority in the processor. Regarding to the trap table, it is shown that only a quarter of all possible hardware trap types are used by the existing implementation. Therefore, it is possible to define new trap types, which can be used by the modified and secure LEON 2 processor core.

Trap	TT	Pri.	Description
reset	0x00	1	Power-On reset
write error	0x2b	2	Write buffer error
instruction_access_error	0x01	3	Error during instruction fetch
illegal_instruction	0x02	5	Un-implemented instruction
privileged_instruction	0x03	4	Priv. instruction in usermode
fp_disabled	0x04	6	FP instr. while FPU disabled
cp_disabled	0x24	6	CP instr. while CP disabled
watchpoint_detected	0x0B	7	Instruction or watchpoint
window_overflow	0x05	8	SAVE into invalid window
window_underflow	0x06	8	RESTORE into invalid window
register_hardware_error	0x20	9	Register file EDAC error
mem_address_not_aligned	0x07	10	Access to un-aligned address
fp_exception	0x08	11	FPU exception
cp_exception	0x28	11	CP exception
data_access_exception	0x09	13	Access error in load or store
tag_overflow	0x0A	14	Tagged arithmetic overflow
divide_exception	0x2A	15	Divide by zero
interrupt_level_1	0x11	31	Asynchronous interrupt 1
interrupt_level_2	0x12	30	Asynchronous interrupt 2
interrupt_level_3	0x13	29	Asynchronous interrupt 3
interrupt_level_4	0x14	28	Asynchronous interrupt 4
interrupt_level_5	0x15	27	Asynchronous interrupt 5
interrupt_level_6	0x16	26	Asynchronous interrupt 6
interrupt_level_7	0x17	25	Asynchronous interrupt 7
interrupt_level_8	0x18	24	Asynchronous interrupt 8
interrupt_level_9	0x19	23	Asynchronous interrupt 9
interrupt_level_10	0x1A	22	Asynchronous interrupt 10
interrupt_level_11	0x1B	21	Asynchronous interrupt 11
interrupt_level_12	0x1C	20	Asynchronous interrupt 12
interrupt_level_13	0x1D	19	Asynchronous interrupt 13
interrupt_level_14	0x1E	18	Asynchronous interrupt 14
interrupt_level_15	0x1F	17	Asynchronous interrupt 15
trap_instruction	0xFF	16	Software trap instruction

Figure 6-20: LEON 2 Trap Table [34]

6.3.3. Trap Base Register

The Trap Base Register (TBR) contains the memory address to which control is transferred when a trap occurs. The trap handler is located at this address. It represents software code, which guarantees the treatment of the particular trap. The TBR consists of the following fields: Trap base address (TBA), Trap type (*tt*) and zero bits (zero). [30]

Traps are indicated by the fact that the hardware writes a unique value into the *tt* field of the TBR. The 8 bits of this field allow 256 distinct types of traps. One half is reserved for hardware and the other half is reserved for software traps, which are caused by the execution of a special instruction. The allocation of the *tt* values to the traps are shown in Figure 6-20.

All possible traps need approximately 4 KBytes memory space, which is called trap table. This memory space is indicated by the address stored in the TBA field. Therefore, it is possible to store the trap table variably in the memory and the supervisor software establishes the location of the trap table automatically. The 4 Least Significant Bits (LSB) of the TBR are used to allocate the different trap handlers to the traps. Therefore, 16 software instructions per trap are possible.

6.3.4. Trap Generation

To handle detected buffer overflows, a new trap type, which is called Out-Of-Bounds exception, has to be inserted in the existing LEON 2 trap table. As a result, a new constant value that is equal to 0x29 (101001) was defined in the *sparcv8.vhd* file. The type definitions are shown in Figure 6-21. In the implementation of the LEON 2 processor the two Most Significant Bits (MSB) of the *tt* field are always zero. Only 6 bits are essential to make a distinction between occurring traps.

```
-- Out-Of-Bound Trap Type, Using Existing Code
constant OOBEXC_TT : std_logic_vector(5 downto 0) := "101010";

-- New (not implemented) Out-Of-Bound Trap Type
constant OOBEXC_TT : std_logic_vector(5 downto 0) := "101001";
```

Figure 6-21: Trap Type Definition

The LEON 2 trap table offers enough memory space, to insert a second trap type. So, it will be possible to differentiate, whether the low or the high bound causes the exception. This enables a more detailed treatment and documentation of exception situations.

The IU is responsible for the generation of the content of TBR. During the memory stage the IU has to detect, which trap is occurred. This mechanism is shown in Figure 6-22.

```
-- Trap Generation: Out-Of-Bound Traps

if ((ctrl.annul or ctrl.trap) /= '1') then

    if((comp_out_low and me.valid_bounds) = '1')
        then ctrl.trap := '1'; ctrl.tt := OOBEXC_TT;
        ...
    elsif ((comp_out_high and me.valid_bounds) = '1')
        then ctrl.trap := '1'; ctrl.tt := OOBEXC_TT;
        ...
    else
        ...

end if;
```

Figure 6-22: Trap Generation in Memory Stage

The results of the two individual comparator units will be analysed, to decide whether a trap occurs or not. If a trap occurred, the bit mask of the particular trap type will be stored in the internal control register of the IU, provided that valid bounds are used for the comparison. In that it can be differentiated, whether the low or the high bound caused the exception. Additionally the trap flag of this register is set, to enable the trap handling in the particular pipeline stage.

6.3.5. Trap Handling

The handling of a trap is done in the write stage of the IU as shown in Figure 6-23. Firstly, the particular trap type is loaded from the control register to keep it non-volatile in the write stage. If a trap occurred, the storage of the PC and an exception bit are enabled. This bit is shifted to the fetch stage to cause the right program jump. During the next step, the final trap address, which consists of the TBA and the previously loaded trap type, is generated. Additionally the storage of the PC will be prepared.

Finally, at the end of the write stage the value of the PC is stored in the local register file. This is necessary to enable the correct restoring of system status, after trap handling is finished.

```
-- Get Trap Type
newtt := "00" & wr.ctrl.tt;

-- Enable Exceptions, Store Program Counter
if ((wr.ctrl.trap and not wr.ctrl.annul) = '1') then
        ...
        exception := '1';
        write_reg := '1'; save_pc := '1';
        ...
end if;

-- Generate Final Trap Address
trap_address(31 downto 4) := sregs.tba & newtt;
trap_address(3 downto PCLOW) := (others => '0');

-- Prepare Storage of Program Counter
if save_pc = '1' then wrdata(31 downto 0) := npc(31 downto 2) & "00";

-- Shift Program Counter to Register File
rfi.wrdata <= wrdata;
rfi.wren <= write_reg;

-- Shift Trap Address to Fetch Stage
fecomb.exception <= exception;
fecomb.trap_address <= trap_address;
```

Figure 6-23: Trap Handling in Write Stage

Triggering out-of-bounds traps is shown in Figure 6-24. This procedure is realised in the memory stage of LEON 2 and used for *LD* instructions only.

```
if(op3 = LD) then
        if ((comp_out_low and me.valid_bounds) = '1')
                then ctrl.trap := '1'; ctrl.tt := OOBEXC_TT;
        elsif ((comp_out_high and me.valid_bounds) = '1')
                then ctrl.trap := '1'; ctrl.tt := OOBEXC_TT;
        end if;
end if;
```

Figure 6-24: Trigger of Out-Of-Bounds Traps

As described in section 3.3, there are two possibilities how to implement trap handling in the SPARC V8 based LEON 2 processor core. One was to use static traps, which means that a fixed trap base address is triggered for each bound violation. The other was to use dynamic traps. In that case, customized trap base addresses are used, which are generated from a try-catch software block. To ease the implementation of the existing processor implementation and to avoid compatibility problems with the operating system, the static trap approach was used.

6.4. Results

The results show how the operation of the final approach can be verified. It includes a simple functionality check, but no performance evaluation. This could not be established, due to restrictions of the software environment. However, simulation based performance results are discussed in section 4.5.

To establish hardware bound checking, it is necessary to store code and data in memory. Most development systems provide programs, which enable to write a particular content directly into the memory. In case of LEON 2, this can be done via GRMON and using the command *load*. With the help of this tool it is possible to load an image to the memory and execute it. For a bound check in hardware, this image had to be adapted in a way that it contains the necessary bound information.

Basically, the source code has to be changed and recompiled, in case of an already existing program. Depending on the size and the complexity of the source code this could be an undefined load of work. Rewriting is costly and time consuming. So, two approaches for testing the functionality of the new technique were worked out. In both approaches, it is necessary to write test programs, but the way how it is loaded is different. Firstly, it is possible to compile user-code directly to machine-code and load it via GRMON into the on-board memory. Secondly, an integration of the test program into an operating system can be performed. In the next step the operating system, will be started and the test program is executed. In both cases, it is necessary that the compiler, which translates a program automatically, inserts the necessary bound information and the bound check instructions. On this way it is possible to insert and use provided bounds.

The method of integrating test programs into an existing operating system was used. Therefore, C/C++ test programs were written and translated to SPARC V8 machine-code. Finally, they were executed on the operating system. To insert the needed bound check information and the needed bound check instructions C/C++ inline assembly commands were used.

So, it was possible to insert SPARC V8 assembler code directly into the C/C++ program. An advantage of the used method is that it is not necessary to perform changes in the compiler yet, because the checking code can be inserted manually.

test_array[0]	0x64	0x1000
test_array[1]	0x65	0x1004
test_array[2]	0x66	0x1008
test_array[3]	0x67	0x100c
test_array[4]	0x68	0x1010
test_array[5]	0x69	0x1014
test_array[6]	0x6a	0x1018
test_array[7]	0x6b	0x101c
test_array[8]	0x6c	0x1020
test_array[9]	0x6d	0x1024
array_start_pointer	0x1000	0x1028
array_end_pointer	0x1024	0x102c

Figure 6-25: Addressing of Test Array

For testing the functionality of the implemented bounds check mechanism, a test array was built up. Ten memory allocations and associated addresses were used, as shown in Figure 6-25. In addition to the content of the array (0x1000 to 0x1024), the associated bounds are stored at memory addresses 0x1028 and 0x1034. To access these two bound values in the assembler, it is also necessary to store their memory addresses, because by means of the assembler, pointer arithmetic is not supported. The values and references of the array, which is used in the test cases, are shown in Figure 6-26.

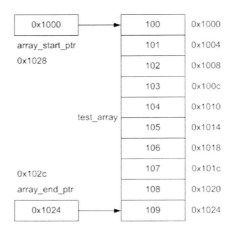

Figure 6-26: Values and References of Test Array

There were different ways to read from the defined array. Firstly, an access does not use the bound check mechanism and has to return a valid value. Secondly, the bounds are loaded and the access is within the bounds. As a result, the access is also valid. Finally, an illegal access to the array happens and this results in a non-valid access.

To use the proposed bound checking technique, it is necessary to load low and high bounds of the array into two global registers, called *%g4* and *%g5*. Due to the fact that the assembler does not know a *LLB* or a *LHB* command, these new load instructions have to be implemented as op-codes. This is done regarding to the definition of a SPARC V8 load integer instruction structure, which is shown in Figure 6-27.

11	rd	op3	rs1	i=0	asi	rs2
31	*29*	*24*	*18*	*13*	*12*	*4* *0*

11	rd	op3	rs1	i=1	simm13
31	*29*	*24*	*18*	*13*	*12* *0*

Figure 6-27: Load Integer Instruction in SPARC V8 [30]

The execution of the test program can be realised in two ways:

- The program can be executed directly on the processor on basis of a sparc-elf-gcc command. For that purpose the existing GRMON environment has to be changed to catch an Out-Of-Bound trap.

- The test program can be integrated into the Linux SnapGear operating system and be executed as an executable file.

Concerning the complexity of the first execution method, it was decided to implement the following programs into the */bin* directory of the Linux SnapGear operating system:

- *test_access_array.exe...* Without bound violation

- *test_low_bound.exe.......* Bound violation, out-of-bounds access

- *test_high_bound.exe .....* Bound violation, out-of-bounds access

- *clear_bounds.exe ....* Clear bound register files

The C source files were compiled to executable files, which contain assembly code that can be directly executed by the target processor core.

```
int main() {
        int return_value;                        int array_size = 10;
        int test_array[array_size];              int *array_start = 0;
        int *array_end = 0;                      int counter = 0;
        int last_array_index = array_size - 1;   array_start = test_array;
        array_end = &(test_array[last_array_index]);

        for (counter = 0; counter < array_size; counter++) {
                test_array[counter] = counter + 100;
        }

        // Insert Load Instructions for Low and High Bounds
        __asm__ ("ld %0, %%g4\n\t"
                "ld %1, %%g5\n\t"
                // 3...FMT3, 8... Output Register 1,  8...Op-Code for LLB
                // 4...Global Register 4, 0...No Offset
                ".long (3<<30)|(8<<25)| (8<<19)|(4<<14)|(0)\n\t"
                // 3...FMT3, 8... Output Register 1, 24...Op-Code for LHB
                // 5...Global Register 4, 0...No Offset
                ".long (3<<30)|(8<<25)|(24<<19)|(5<<14)|(0)"
                : /* no output registers */
                :"g"(array_start), "g"(array_end)
                :"memory"
                );

        // Read from an Element of the Array (index 0)
        return_value = test_array[0];
        return return_value;
}
```

Figure 6-28: Excerpt of Test Program

To ease the trap handling in the current implementation an already implemented trap with a *Illegal Instruction* (trap code 0x02) exception was used to show an occurring bound violation. The test program, which is shown in Figure 6-28, is used to test the final implementation of the Secure CPU. Only the array access (highlighted as bold) has to be modified to create valid or out-of-bounds system states, which was done in the several test programs.

Figure 6-29 illustrates the output of GRMON including loading the file *test_high_bound.exe*, the *run* command, as well as an excerpt of the instruction tracing (for the last 12 assembler instructions). The outputs *unknown opcode*, stand for the additionally implemented instructions *LLB* and *LHB*, because they are not registered in this version of GRMON.

```
grlib> load test_high_bound.exe
          section: .text at 0x40000000, size 39888 bytes
          section: .data at 0x40009bd0, size 2844 bytes
          total size: 42732 bytes (83.8 kbit/s)
          read 140 symbols
          entry point: 0x40000000

grlib> run
IU in error mode     (tt = 0x02)
40000020  91d02000   ta  0x0

grlib> inst 12
       time      address    instruction                      result
       8671893   400012d0   ld   [%fp - 0x14], %g4           [43ffff20]
       8671901   400012d4   ld   [%fp - 0x18], %g5           [43ffff44]
       8671902   400012d8   unknown opcode: 0xd0410000       [43ffff20]
       8671903   400012dc   unknown opcode: 0xd0c14000       [43ffff44]
       8671904   400012e0   nop                              [00000000]
       8671905   400012e4   nop                              [00000000]
       8671906   400012e8   nop                              [00000000]
       8671907   400012ec   nop                              [00000000]
       8671909   400012f0   nop                              [00000000]
       8671910   400012f4   nop                              [00000000]
       8671918   400012f8   ld   [%fp - 0x28], %o2           [43ffff20]
       8671927   400012fc   ld   [%o2 + 0x28], %o0           [trapped]
```

Figure 6-29: GRMON Output with Bound Violation

Concluding, it was possible to execute all test programs on the developed secure processor architecture. Examples that include bound violations could be trapped, as shown in the last line of Figure 6-29. Also legacy code, like an operating system, could be executed successfully, because the trapping mechanism was disabled due to the missing bound information.

Conclusion

The main idea of the book "Secure CPU" was to develop a processor core extension that provides an improved capability against software vulnerabilities and improves the security of target systems passively. The architecture directly executes bound checking in hardware without performance loss, whereas checking in software would make any application intolerably slow. Based on new concepts of byte-code and intermediate languages, which support data-type information within meta data at the intermediate language level, changes would be shifted to the last step in the compilation process. Simulation results demonstrated that the proposed design offers a higher performance and security, when compared to other solutions. For the implementation of the Secure CPU, the SPARC V8 based LEON 2 processor from Gaisler Research was used. The processor core was adapted and finally synthesised for a GR-XC3S-1500 board and extended, as explained in this book.

The design is not specialised for a specific target market or region. However it could be most effectively used in applications, especially where the passive security is a major topic. As more embedded systems influence human life, such as medical or automotive systems, this topic gets increasingly important. The customer will benefit of a faster time-to-market for systems with highly improved security without additional efforts. The final architecture reduces the time for the application development and fastens the hardware requirements specification process, because security can be tested in advance. As a consequence, system testing will be eased and speeded up as well. Examples have shown that VHDL code actually is producible as custom chip, thus avoiding the higher costs of FPGAs in higher quantities.

The proposed ideas, simulations and implementations were published in several international conference and workshop proceedings, as well as in selected journals all around the world. The associated work was published in [41], [42], [43], [44], [45], [46] and [47].

References

[1]   Wheeler D., Countering buffer overflows, Secure Programmer, IBM, January 27, 2004.

[2]   development.tecChannel, Basiswissen Buffer Overflow, IDG Business Media, May 4, 2004.

[3]   Inoue K., Secure Cache: Run-Time Detection and Prevention of Buffer Overflow Attacks, Proceedings of the Asia and South Pacific International Conference on Embedded SoCs, July, 2005.

[4]   Lee R., Karig D., McGregor J. and Shi Z., Enlisting Hardware Architecture to Thwart Malicious Code Injection, Proceedings of International Conference on Security in Pervasive Computing, Boppard, Germany, March, 2003.

[5]   Inoue K., Energy-Security Tradeoff in a Secure Cache Architecture Against Buffer Overflow Attacks, ACM SIGARCH Computer Architecture News, Volume 33, Issue 1, March, 2005.

[6]   Piotrowski M., Festung Linux – eine Übersicht von Projekten, hakin9 Nr. 2/2006, February, 2006.

[7]   Klein T., Buffer Overflows und Format-String-Schwachstellen, dpunkt verlag, 2004.

[8]   IBM, Stack-Smashing Protector, November 8, 2000.

[9]   Litchfield D., Defeating the Stack Based Buffer Overflow Prevention Mechanism of Microsoft Windows 2003 Server, NGSSoftware Insight Security Research, September 8, 2003.

[10]   Ren C., Weber M. and McGraw G., Microsoft Compiler Flaw Technical Note, Cigital, February 14, 2002.

[11]   Jones R. and Kelly P., Backwards-compatible bounds checking for arrays and pointers in C programs, International Workshop on Automated Debugging, Linköping, Sweden, May, 1997.

[12]   Cowan C., Pu C., Maier D., Walpole J. and Bakke P., StackGuard: Automatic Adaptive Detection and Prevention of Buffer-Overflow Attacks, Proceedings of 7th USENIX Security Symposium, San Antonio, Texas, USA, January, 1998.

[13]   Ruwase O. and Lam M., A Practical Dynamic Buffer Overflow Detector, Proceedings of the 11th Annual Network and Distributed System Security Symposium, San Diego, California, February, 2004.

[14]   Rinard M., Cadar., Dumitran D., Roy D. and Leu T., A Dynamic Technique for Eliminating Buffer Overflow Vulnerabilities (and Other Memory Errors), Proceedings of 20th Annual Computer Security Applications Conference, Tucson, Arizona, USA, December, 2004.

[15]   Xu J., Kalbarczyk Z., Patel S. and Iyer R., Architecture Support for Defending Against Buffer Overflow Attacks, 2nd Workshop on Evaluating and Architecting System dependabilitY, San Jose, California, USA, October 6, 2002.

[16]   Chiueh T. and Hsu F., RAD: A Compile-Time Solution to Buffer Overflow Attacks, Proceedings of 21st IEEE International Conference on Distributed Computing Systems, Phoenix, Arizona, USA April, 2001.

[17]   Anglefire.com, StackShield, January 7, 2000.

[18]   Madan B., Phoha S. and Trivedi K., StackOFFence: A Technique for Defending Against Buffer Overflow Attacks, International Conference on Information Technology: Coding and Computing, Las Vegas, Nevada, USA, April 6, 2005.

[19]   Paulson L., New Chips Stop Buffer Overflow Attacks, Computer Volume 37 of IEEE Computer Society, October, 2004.

[20]   Enderle R. and Noel J., The New Approach to Windows Security, Advanced Micro Devices and Enderle Group, June 25, 2004.

[21]   Kuo S., Execute Disable Bit Functionality Blocks Malware Code Execution, Intel Software Networks, June, 2004.

[22]   Andersen S. and Abella V., Changes to Functionality in Microsoft Windows XP Service Pack 2, Part 3: Memory Protection Technologies, Microsoft TechnNet, August 9, 2004.

[23]   Advanced Micro Devices, AMD64 Architecture Programmer's Manual Volume 2: System Programming, Revision 3.12, September, 2006.

[24]   Miller M., Bypassing PatchGuard on Windows x64, Uniformed.org, December 1, 2005.

[25]   Miller M., Bypassing Windows Hardware-enforced Data Execution Prevention, Uniformed.org, October 2, 2005.

[26]   Lam L. and Chiuch T., Checking Array Bound Violation Using Segmentation Hardware, Proceedings of International Conference on Dependable Systems and Networks, Yokohama, Japan, June, 2005.

[27]   Shao Z. et al, Efficient Array & Pointer Bound Checking Against Buffer Overflow Attacks via Hardware/Software, IEEE International Conference on Information Technology: Coding and Computing, Las Vegas, USA, April 4 to 6, 2005.

[28]   Shao Z., Zhuge, Q., He Y. and Sha E., Defending Embedded Systems against Buffer Overflow via Hardware/Software, 19th Annual Computer Security Applications Conference, Storrs, USA, December, 2003.

[29]   Shao Z. et al, Security Protection and Checking for Embedded System Integration against Buffer Overflow Attacks via Hardware/Software, IEEE Transactions on Computers, Volume 55, Issue 4, April, 2006.

[30]   SPARC International Inc., The SPARC Architecture Manual Version 8, Revision SAV080SI9308, 1992.

[31]   Reinert D., Von-Neumann-CPU-Simulator, Ruhr-Universität Bochum, Bochum, Germany, May 28, 2006

[32]   Gumm H.P. and Perner M., Der CPU-Simulator MikroSim, Marburg, Germany, May 28, 2006

[33]   Skrien D., CPUSim 3.1: A Tool for Simulating Computer Architectures for Computer Organization Classes, ACM Journal of Educational Resources in Computing, Volume 1, Issue 4, December, 2001.

[34]   Gaisler J., LEON 2 Processor User's Manual XST Edition, Version 1.0.30, Gaisler Research, Göteborg, Sweden, July, 2005.

[35]   Gaisler J., GRMON User's Manual, Version 1.1.13d, Gaisler Research, Göteborg, Sweden, July, 2006

[36]   Xilinx, XSV Board V1.1 Manual – How to install and use your new XSV Board, September 21, 2001.

[37]   Xilinx, Virtex 2.5 V Field Programmable Gate Arrays – Product Specification, DS003, Version 2.5, Xilinx, April 2, 2001

[38]   XESS Corporation, XSV800 schematic drawing Version 1.1, 2006.

[39]   Gaisler Research/Pender Electronics Design, GR-XC3S-1500 Development Board – User Manual Version 1.1, May 29, 2006.

[40]   Xilinx, Spartan-3 FPGA Family: Complete Data Sheet, Product Specification DS099, Version 2.1, April 26, 2006.

[41]   Grasser M.G. and Brenner E., Efficient Hardware Bound Checking Against Buffer Overflow Attacks to Improve Security in Computer Systems, Proceedings of the International Conference on Intelligent and Information Systems, Varazdin, Croatia, September 20, 2006.

[42]   Grasser M.G. and Brenner E., Security Improvement in Embedded Systems via an Efficient Hardware Bound Checking Architecture, Proceedings of MoMM2006 & iiWAS2006 Workshops, Yogyakarta, Indonesia, December 4, 2006.

[43]   Grasser M.G. and Brenner E., Defence of Embedded Systems Against Buffer Overflow Attacks via a Secure Processor Architecture, Proceedings of Embedded World Conference, Nurnberg, Germany, February 15, 2007.

[44] Grasser M.G., Embedded Security Solution for Digital Safe-Guard Ecosystems, Proceedings of Inaugural IEEE International Digital Ecosystems and Technologies Conference, Cairns, Australia, February 21-23, 2007.

[45] Grasser M.G., Priebsch J., Hofer G. and Brenner E., Powerful Hardware Bound Checking in Embedded Systems via a Secure Processor Architecture and Secure Bound Storage, Proceedings of IADIS International Conference Applied Computing, Salamanca, Spain, February 18-20, 2007.

[46] Grasser M.G. and Brenner E., SecureCPU – Eine sichere Prozessorarchitektur für den Einsatz in mobilen und eingebetteten Systemen, Forschungsjournal der Technischen Universität Graz, Graz, Austria, 2007.

[47] Grasser M.G., Priebsch J., Hofer G. and Hodanek T., Simulation of a Secure CPU with Secure Tag to Defend Embedded Systems Against Buffer Overflow Attacks, Proceedings of ACS/IEEE International Conference on Computer Systems and Applications, Amman, Jordan, May 13-16, 2007.

Printed in the United States
126436LV00002B/41/P